Still Making
Waves

Still Making Waves

Creating a Splash
in Midlife & Beyond

Gracie Malone

Revell

Grand Rapids, Michigan

Published by Fleming H. Revell
a division of Baker Publishing Group
P.O. Box 6287, Grand Rapids, MI 49516-6287
www.revellbooks.com

Printed in the United States of America

Library of Congress Cataloging-in-Publication Data
Malone, Gracie.
    Still making waves : creating a splash in midlife & beyond / Gracie
Malone.
        p.   cm.
    Includes bibliographical references.
    ISBN 0-8007-5851-X (pbk.)
    1. Middle aged women—Religious life. I. Title.
BV4579.5.M345 2004
248.8′43—dc22   2004009237

To my three sons:
Matt, Mike, and Jason—
Thanks for loving me even when I call you
by the wrong name
and tell stories about you—over and over and over again.
I realize being friends with a doting mother
now that you are all grown up
is a choice—maybe even a hard one—
so I'm overwhelmed and delighted to be
included in your circle of friendship
and able to celebrate life with you.
Thank you for being men who forgive quickly,
love unconditionally, and laugh heartily.
I love you dearly.

Contents

CONTENTS

Foreword

Earplugs and nurturing grace. These two factors have shaped my love and admiration for author and girl-friend Gracie Malone.

Let's start with the earplugs.

Several years ago I asked Gracie, then an acquaintance, to room with me during a winter writer's conference in sunny Florida. Trust me, I don't take roommates lightly—six days with the wrong person can be excruciatingly painful. But our personalities had clicked well during a prior conference. We shared a mutual love for inductive Bible study (something you don't come across every day), and Gracie had made me snort out loud with laughter. That was before we were to meet in Florida and before I had gained about twelve pounds—twelve pounds (and I would testify to this in court) that settled in my throat and nasal passages. This triggered some serious air passage problems that resulted in my snoring for the first time in my life.

I'm talking snoring with a capital S, snoring that my children enthusiastically reenacted while seated at our kitchen table (which I crawled underneath), that forced my six-foot-one-inch husband out of our bedroom and onto a five-foot-five-inch sofa in our living room, and that absolutely mortified me—and that was around my family. There was no way I'd be able to face Gracie, a mere acquaintance, after a night of such horrible snoring.

I decided to cancel my journey south. Unable to gather the courage to call, I opted for a cowardly email instead:

Dear Gracie,

I hate to tell you this but here goes—it looks like I'm going to have to cancel my trip to Florida. I've had some unexpected things occur, and it's probably best if I stay home. I'm so sorry!

Love,
Julie

Within minutes came this reply:

Dear Julie,

Drat! I was looking forward to getting to know you better. Didn't you purchase your ticket already? That's nonrefundable, right? I don't mean to be nosey, but if you're a little tight on cash, I'd be happy to put the hotel expense on my credit card, and you can pay me your part whenever you have it to give. Let's try and work this all out no matter what the unexpected thing may be!

Love,
Gracie

I don't know what sort of response I expected, but Gracie's thoughtfulness and willingness to deal with the matter at hand sent a wave of relief and resolve through my spirit. I decided to confess my sordid secret.

Dear Gracie,

You are such a sweetheart! Okay, I'm going to be totally honest about The Problem. The reason I can't attend the conference is . . . I've gained TONS of weight, and I now snore louder than a Burlington Northern freight train. (Embarrassed sigh.) I don't think I can lose twelve pounds in four days. I don't want to keep you awake for five nights in a row. And I find this all so embarrassing that I believe I'll just melt into a puddle of shame right now!

Your shallow and nasally impaired friend,
Julie

When my phone rang moments after I had hit Send, I knew who was going to be on the other end.

"Is that all?" Gracie asked with nary a hello or introduction. "Well, listen to me, don't you think another thought of it. I just happen to own a pair of Air Force Stealth-Fighter pilot-approved earplugs, and all I have to do is pop one in each ear, pull the covers over my tired body, and sleep like a baby!" With a warm chuckle, she added, "I do ask that you wake me up if a fire alarm sounds or a hurricane sneaks up on us."

Gracie made it that easy.

In our "reach out and touch" long distance moment, she extended a nurturing grace (Friendship Factor No. 2), which officially catapulted our relationship from acquaintance to girlfriend status.

I attended the conference, Gracie used her earplugs, and we had the most marvelous time together that you can possibly imagine. But the kicker? The coup de grace when it comes to Gracie's character? She never said a word of this to any of the other women attending the meeting. Not a sarcastic remark was made. Not a pun expressed at my snoring expense.

With the same grace, and a liberal dose of postmeno-pausal wit and sass, Gracie has written what I believe to be her finest book yet. *Still Making Waves* is my Texan friend's bold declaration that life in the second half is to be lived, embraced, and seized.

Whoo ha!

I'm so thankful for Gracie, who proves—through her own tales of laughter and loss, joy and sorrow, fulfillment and regret—that there is a priceless payoff for staying young at heart.

If you can, clear your busy schedule for an hour or two of reading pleasure, or get a chapter or two in between golf games and grandchildren's visits. Be it little by little or in one fell swoop, you'll come to appreciate and love Gracie's humor, charm, integrity, and authentic voice of challenge just as I have, along with other family, friends, and reading fans.

And, oh yes, one last reminder: Fasten your seat belts, because *Still Making Waves* promises to be a bumpy and gloriously exhilarating ride!

Julie Ann Barnhill

Introduction

In April 2000 I celebrated a millennial milestone of my own: the Big Six Oh! birthday. Although it was not the traumatic event I expected, the occasion caused me to take a good, hard look at my future. *Was my life half-lived already? What did I want to accomplish in my second half of life? What could I begin in midlife?* (Yes, I said "midlife," for I intend to live to be at least 100 or maybe even 120!)

About that time, I found myself browsing through the cards in one of my favorite gift stores. A particular birthday card leaped off the rack at me. It pictured four women in bright, colorful bathing suits, their bodies in various stages of droop. They stood holding hands, facing the waves with their toes in the sand, ready to take a plunge into the cool waters of the deep blue sea.

I giggled as I headed to the cash register—a birthday card from me to me.

Even though the picture on the card was a real hoot, it tugged at my heart with a deeper message. I want to be one of those women, holding hands with others, finding courage and support and having fun as we face an ocean full of life's challenges. I want to stand with sisters, toes in the sand, drawing strength from each other and from God. And because I've drifted into a few turbulent seas in life and from time to time waded into some rather deep waters of my own, I want to be one of those women to you—to come alongside and say, "C'mon, let's face the waves of life together."

Who hasn't, from time to time, felt pulled out to sea by a current or been swept off her feet by fierce gales and a forceful wave?

Maybe you are still trying to balance the competing demands of a job, family, and social obligations. Perhaps now the kids are grown and gone, with children of their own, and you've found it's not much fun coping with the empty nest or a retired husband at your heels, always rearranging your spice cabinet. Or you could be wondering what use you are to anyone, all the while coping with the reality of turkey-neck wrinkles and baggy biceps.

Certainly I have days when I can swim like a champ, making real headway through the gulf streams of life. But with each new birthday, there are more frequent moments that challenge. At times I feel like I'm doing the backstroke in a stagnant pool or floating aimlessly on my back in an ocean of mistakes and missteps. I find I more often need to look up toward heaven for some direction.

Whatever the case, I'm determined to stay afloat. I will not "go gentle into that good night." I don't want to fizzle out but to create sparks like a firecracker for those around me—maybe while wearing scarlet and purple.

Are you ready to stop existing and begin living it up? Consider this book a friend who says, "Here's your chance to start over." It can begin with chapter 1 and however old you are today.

So what are you waiting for? Run (or waddle or mosey or whatever you can do) and pull on your bathing suit. Then meet me where the sand of today meets the ocean of tomorrow; grab my hand, and together we'll jump into the invigorating waters of Life, Part Two. You're never too old to begin again, and it's never too late to *start making some waves.*

PART 1

It's Never Too Late for
a Happy Childhood

1

Launching into New Depths

~∽

MAKING PEACE WITH THE PAST

There is no need to plead that the love of God shall fill our hearts as though He were unwilling to fill us. His love is pressing around us on all sides like air. Cease to resist, and instantly love takes possession.

Amy Carmichael

One evening during a special service in our church, a teenage girl named Lindsay stood and walked to the microphone. In an animated voice peppered with teen jargon, she said, "I like to think about God as my daddy. To call him 'Father' just seems . . . too formal or something. He's my Dad."

I leaned forward in my seat, feeling that this girl had a message I really needed to hear.

The concept of God being my heavenly Father always left me feeling a little ambiguous. My all-too-earthly dad could have been the prototype for either of the lead characters in the movie *Grumpy Old Men*. Dad was a grouch with a sense of humor, but living with such a dual personality can be frightening for a little girl. Before I was even old enough to go to school, I had to learn to cope with my father's "irregular" personality—a skill that serves me well even to this day.

When Dad came home from work, I never knew which side of him would come through the door. Around 5:30 on weekdays, gravel popped beneath the wheels of Dad's pickup when he pulled in our driveway. I would run to the window, push back the curtains, and watch him get out of his truck. It was always the same routine: He gathered his newspaper, lunch box, and hat. Then he trudged down the planks toward our back door. If he sauntered toward the house with a grin on his face, I knew he was in a good mood with a funny story to tell. I'd greet him at the door and help Mother clean out his lunch box, and we'd sit at the kitchen table, sipping tall glasses of iced tea, listening and laughing as Dad spun a tale. But if he stomped down the walkway, red faced and sullen, I'd head for the back room and get lost in a book or slip out the front door to go ride my bicycle.

I could read my daddy's emotional temperature as easily as the thermostat on our old Dearborn heater.

As I matured, I learned that between my dad's grumpy-old-man side and his happy-go-lucky side, there was some middle ground, like a sandbar in the midst of a roaring river. In that turning point, I could appeal to my father's sense of humor and turn the tide of his emotions from a raging current into a peaceful stream.

The first time I remember this happening, I had literally destroyed one of the new trees he'd planted along the driveway. Since we didn't have a gym set, the small tree had to suffice. All afternoon my little brother Harold and I swung round and round on its trunk and dangled from its tiny branches. (I don't know where in the world my mother was during this escapade.)

The beleaguered tree actually held up fairly well until I tried a trick I'd seen a clown perform at the Farmers Branch Carnival. I thought that by placing my hands just right on the trunk of the tree, I could swing my body into a horizontal position and flutter there like a flag on a windy day. I placed one hand near the ground and the other about two feet higher. When I tried to hoist my chubby little body sideways into the air, the trunk of the tree splintered and crumpled like a Chinese finger puzzle.

Harold threw up his hands and headed for the house, shouting over his shoulder as he ran, "It's not my fault! It's not my fault!"

Not being one to give up easily, I decided I could patch up that tree so nobody would ever know what we'd done. I squeezed its trunk back together and plastered the bark in place with a handful of mud. I thought I'd done a dandy job, but by the time Dad pulled in the driveway, the leaves on his little tree had begun to wilt like tea leaves in hot water . . . and speaking of hot water, I was about to be up to my ears in it.

My heart pounded as Dad burst through the back door and began looking for me. He found me in our living room, stretched out on the sofa, my face buried in a comic book.

21

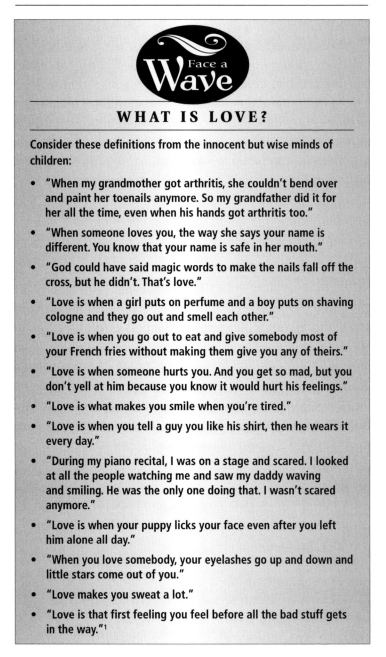

WHAT IS LOVE?

Consider these definitions from the innocent but wise minds of children:

- "When my grandmother got arthritis, she couldn't bend over and paint her toenails anymore. So my grandfather did it for her all the time, even when his hands got arthritis too."
- "When someone loves you, the way she says your name is different. You know that your name is safe in her mouth."
- "God could have said magic words to make the nails fall off the cross, but he didn't. That's love."
- "Love is when a girl puts on perfume and a boy puts on shaving cologne and they go out and smell each other."
- "Love is when you go out to eat and give somebody most of your French fries without making them give you any of theirs."
- "Love is when someone hurts you. And you get so mad, but you don't yell at him because you know it would hurt his feelings."
- "Love is what makes you smile when you're tired."
- "Love is when you tell a guy you like his shirt, then he wears it every day."
- "During my piano recital, I was on a stage and scared. I looked at all the people watching me and saw my daddy waving and smiling. He was the only one doing that. I wasn't scared anymore."
- "Love is when your puppy licks your face even after you left him alone all day."
- "When you love somebody, your eyelashes go up and down and little stars come out of you."
- "Love makes you sweat a lot."
- "Love is that first feeling you feel before all the bad stuff gets in the way."[1]

"What did you do to my tree?" he yelled. "You kids . . ."

I knew I had to stop him, so I launched into a lengthy explanation of the complicated chain of events, hoping with every detail that I would spot just one teensy sign that he might find a smidgen of humor in the situation. It wasn't until I got to the "remember that clown at the carnival?" part that I saw the lines around his mouth relax.

I took a deep breath and dove on into the calming yet still turbulent waters. "Oh, Daddy, I tried so hard to fix your tree. Please don't be mad. You don't want me to run away and join the carnival, do you?"

He shook his head, and just a trace of a grin crossed his lips. "Nope. They'd send you back home before you'd tear down the tent!"

I breathed a huge sigh of relief as he huffed out of the room. Perhaps in a day or two, Dad and I would be laughing about that tree. But at that moment I was just glad to have sidestepped his wrath. While my tactics worked on that occasion, I wouldn't fare so well on others. Sometimes my dad would completely lose control of his temper, and there was nothing funny about it. He'd lash out at me and say hurtful things or make derogatory comments that stunned me, leaving me speechless.

Memories of my father were interrupted by the soft sound of Lindsay shifting from one foot to the other. Pushing her hands deep into her jean pockets, she was saying, "I can just, you know, sit on my heavenly Father's lap and talk to him about anything. Sometimes I write my prayers, like love letters to God." She paused and smiled shyly. "I think he keeps what I've written, sort of like parents keep their kids' crayon drawings. Maybe God puts my prayers on his refrigerator, and when he has company, he says, 'See that prayer? My little girl wrote that for me.'" She then broke into an irrepressible grin. "That's how much God loves me."

Warm tears trickled down my cheeks while Lindsay turned toward her seat. I dabbed my eyes with a tissue, and I thought about the years I'd struggled with having a consistent, compassionate concept of God, a concept that came so easily to Lindsay. Even though it's been a lifetime since I was a little girl looking for approval and love, tears still burn my eyes when I think about God being my daddy.

make a Splash

WHAT'S ON YOUR REFRIGERATOR DOOR?

Display these notes as fun ideas on how to make peace with the past—and present:

- A messy kitchen is a happy kitchen, and this kitchen is delirious.
- If we are what we eat, then I'm easy, fast, and cheap.
- A balanced diet is a cookie in each hand.
- Thou shalt not weigh more than thy refrigerator.
- Blessed are they who can laugh at themselves, for they shall never cease to be amused.
- A clean house is a sign of a misspent life.
- Housework done properly can kill you.
- Countless numbers of people have eaten in this kitchen and gone on to lead normal lives.
- My next house will have no kitchen—just vending machines.

However, on this occasion, my wacky sense of humor didn't allow me to bob about in deep philosophical waters for long. I felt a giggle gurgling up to the surface as I contemplated what God's refrigerator must look like: I imagined myself peering into heaven's kitchen, Jack-in-the-Beanstalk style, and viewing a refrigerator the size of the Empire State Building. God, after all, must have a lot of crayon drawings and prayers to post.

I straightened my face before walking to the front of the room for my turn at the mic. "Maybe some of you are thinking there are no refrigerators in heaven," I said, "but we won't know for sure until he invites us for breakfast, will we?"

The congregation (thankfully) laughed in response. "Seriously, he could have a gigantic refrigerator. He's been known to use tangible things to teach us spiritual truth. The Bible says God collects our tears in a bottle and that he's written the names of every single one of his children in a book. Our heavenly Father treasures Lindsay's love letters, just as he values yours and mine. Who's to say whether or not our love letters and works of heart are posted on a refrigerator that would make Paul Bunyan proud?"

As I left the meeting and headed home, my thoughts turned to my dad again, remembering when he became seriously ill. As a dutiful, middle-aged daughter, I had visited my parents regularly to help with the additional chores and stresses they faced as Dad's disabilities increased. The visits were helpful to my mother, but no matter what I did, I couldn't please my dad. His disapproving glances, the curl of his lip, or a furrowed brow stirred up old feelings, making me feel unacceptable and unloved. Daddy died before I had a chance to resolve my long-held feelings of rejection.

Years later I decided to visit the cemetery where he was buried. I had some things to say, and I knew he couldn't say anything back! For almost an hour I paced, talked, and prayed. I picked at the grass around his tombstone and rearranged the faded plastic mums. Then I stomped the ground and cried, "I needed you! I needed you to accept me, to gather me in your arms each night and hold me close. Did you even really love me? Were you capable of loving your little girl? Yes, we had some good times and some laughs, but I never even once heard you say 'I love you.'"

As I left the cemetery at sunset and drove down the lonely Texas highway toward home, God spoke to my heart: *I'll be your Daddy.*

I swallowed hard, trying to control my emotions as I pondered the implications. What my earthly father could not do because of his own brokenness, God, the awesome Creator of the universe, did for me when he accepted me into his family. For the first time I understood, really understood, what it meant to be a child of God. I pictured my heavenly Father smiling at me—not with some sort of feigned good humor, but because he genuinely loved me just as I was. I felt completely free from the need to perform, to be charming or cute to earn a place of favor with him. I was loved, deeply loved, simply because I was his daughter.

The thought of that kind of unconditional love was more than I could handle and still drive my car. Blinded by tears, I somehow managed to pull onto the shoulder of the road, where I sobbed uncontrollably, releasing years of pent-up emotion into the gentle hands of my heavenly Dad.

Today, decades since that epiphanal moment, I often refer to God as my Abba, an intimate Aramaic word that means "daddy" or "papa."

One day recently, I sat outside on my patio and listed all the reasons that I love my Abba. I wrote my thoughts in a journal, sort of like a love letter to God. First, I listed my Abba's unconditional, everlasting love. He loves me consistently, whether I am lovable or not, even when I sin or make mistakes. Next, I listed his faithfulness. He is always available, always helpful. I noted my Abba's goodness, kindness, and patience. After that I recorded his grace, mercy, and truth.

When I finished my list, my heart seemed strangely connected with my heavenly Father. I breathed a prayer of thanksgiving for the way he meets every single one of my needs.

Then in a moment of spiritual insight, it seemed as if God was speaking back to me. I didn't hear an audible voice, but deep in my heart in that special place where God communicates with the human soul, I heard him say: *I hear you, Gracie, and I'm crazy about you too. I'm going right to the kitchen to put your love note on my refrigerator door.*

Sometimes I wonder how many women have had experiences similar to mine. Perhaps today, thirty or forty years later, you are still nursing hurts and fears left over from years of childhood abuse or neglect. Unfortunately, our wounded feelings and insecurities do not vanish with the passing of time. But there is room for every wounded child, even the gray-headed ones, in the lap of our eternal Father. He hugs with everlasting arms, and I think that means he has arms big enough to go around lots of really big kids.

2

Where Have All the Grown-Ups Gone?

❦

HANDLING ROLE REVERSALS

Age doesn't always bring wisdom, sometimes age comes alone.

Barbara Johnson

Before the days of interstate highways, seventy-miles per-hour speed limits, and protective car seats, a mother's strong arm was the only barrier between her babies and the windshield. When we rounded a corner or screeched to a stop, our arms flew out like stop signs on a school bus. As a result, every mother of my generation developed an impressive bicep in her right arm, and most kids had permanent indentations in their little chests. For me, it's been a habit hard to break.

One day I careened around a corner in downtown Grapevine, Texas, and instinctively flung out my arm, hitting my twenty-three-year-old son Jason smack in the chest. As he sucked in a gulp of air, he bellowed, "Mom, you scared the bejeebers out of me!"

"I'm sorry, honey," I replied absentmindedly, while I eyed the quaint canopied doorsteps on the historic storefronts. Seconds later I slammed on the brakes and smacked him again.

"If you don't stop looking in store windows," Jason yelled, "you're going to get us both killed."

I reeled in my right arm and tucked my fingers under my leg to stop the automatic flinging action. "Jason, to this day I've never caused a wreck, never even had a ticket. I'm a great driver!"

My son shook his head and muttered, "But, Mom, I've heard that as a person, um . . . well, matures, they don't react as quickly as they once did. One second off your response time and you're gonna be toast."

We both laughed as I wheeled on down the road. But I couldn't help wondering, *Now, who is the parent here?*

I realize I'm not the only woman living in the second half of life who has found herself switching roles with a member of the younger generation. In fact, all sorts of role-reversal situations take place as we morph from one stage of life to another. Well-loved humorist Erma Bombeck told about a pivotal point in her life when she realized she was transitioning from a well-cared-for daughter into a caregiver. As the story goes, her mother was sitting in the passenger side of the car when Erma had to make a sudden stop at a traffic light. Instinctively Erma threw out her right arm to keep the older lady from hitting the windshield. This scene must have been similar to others that eventually caused the beloved writer to admit that the metamorphosis was complete. In a newspaper column, she confessed, "My shoulders slumped as I realized that I had just come full circle. I had turned into my mother."[1]

The episode I had with Jason reminded me of a similar incident that had happened a few years before—this time with my five-year-old grandson Luke. On this occasion I was once again tooling around town in my car, paying more attention to my surroundings than the task at hand. I had picked up Luke at school, had buckled him safely in the backseat, and was heading toward town. On a long stretch of scenic road, I found myself daydreaming, until I realized we were approaching a curve. In my quick estimation, it seemed a gentle curve, one that didn't require any drastic decrease in speed. I rounded the curve with my vehicle completely under control, or so I thought.

Luke felt differently. His voice boomed louder than the praise choruses on the radio. "Slow down, Grandma Gracie! You're driving too fast." Then he slapped his hand on his forehead and moaned, "I'd hate for anything to happen to you."

At first Luke's warning struck me as kind of funny. What could a kindergarten kid tell a midlife grandma about driving a car? Nonetheless, he had taken on the adult role, dispensing parentlike wisdom to me, and I felt like a kid in big trouble. My mind was still drafting a snappy comeback when I realized Luke was genuinely concerned—not for his own safety but for mine. What could I do but apologize?

"I'm sorry, Luke," I said contritely. "Next time I'll be more careful." Then, to show I was still the Grown-Up in Charge, I flung my right arm over the seat and patted him on the knee.

"You worry too much, Luke. To this day I've never caused a wreck, never even had a ticket. I'm a great driver!"

I was proud of my sterling driving record. Unfortunately, it eventually became tarnished when I got a ticket—for speeding! And not for zipping along on scenic country back roads either. Oh no! I was ticketed for speeding through a school zone. My first thought was that I, compassionate mother of three, grandmother of six, could have possibly endangered a child. My second thought was, *How can I keep Jason and Luke from finding out about this?*

A few weeks later I signed up for Defensive Driving Online—an Internet course. I figured this to be the most expedient way to purge my driving record of the awful offense, and as a side benefit, my family would never have to know about my misconduct. I registered for the course and got started early one morning.

It would take six hours of instruction, complete with streaming videos and graphic photos, to reprogram my brain and turn me into a safer, slower driver. (If only I had listened to Luke!) The course's introductory remarks made me cringe: "As a smart, rational person, you can learn about your actions and make radical changes in the way you drive."

When I got to the section on speeding, Luke's prophetic words of wisdom came back to haunt me. "It is easy to lose control of your car on a curve," the instructor claimed, "especially when you fail to take into account kinetic energy and centrifugal force." As I maneuvered my mouse on its pad and watched the car on my monitor slide toward a ditch, I had to admit I had never, not even once in my long driving history, even thought about kinetic energy or centrifugal force when rounding a corner. I was a failure at curves.

I also failed to graduate Defensive Driving Online anonymously. For just as I finished a fifteen-minute segment on signs and was heading into a forty-minute section on alcohol-related crashes, my hubby walked through the door and realized what I was doing. After all, nobody takes Defensive Driving unless they've received a ticket. His very first words were, "I'm telling!"

Thankfully, I survived the online driving instruction as well as the family scandal and went on to other learning experiences.

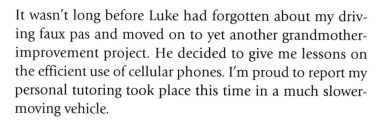

It wasn't long before Luke had forgotten about my driving faux pas and moved on to yet another grandmother-improvement project. He decided to give me lessons on the efficient use of cellular phones. I'm proud to report my personal tutoring took place this time in a much slower-moving vehicle.

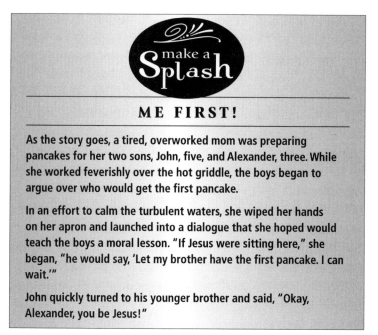

make a Splash

ME FIRST!

As the story goes, a tired, overworked mom was preparing pancakes for her two sons, John, five, and Alexander, three. While she worked feverishly over the hot griddle, the boys began to argue over who would get the first pancake.

In an effort to calm the turbulent waters, she wiped her hands on her apron and launched into a dialogue that she hoped would teach the boys a moral lesson. "If Jesus were sitting here," she began, "he would say, 'Let my brother have the first pancake. I can wait.'"

John quickly turned to his younger brother and said, "Okay, Alexander, you be Jesus!"

I had loaded my grandkids in the car and was driving toward the park when I realized I needed to phone home. I dialed the number and got Jason on the line. After I finished my conversation, I asked five-year-old Luke if he wanted to say hi to his uncle. He did! They chatted a few minutes before Luke said good-bye and pushed the End button.

As I drove on down the road, Luke appeared to be in deep thought as he cradled the phone in his hand. Then the inquisition began. "Grandma Gracie, how much does it cost to talk on a cell phone?"

I knew precisely where this conversation was headed, for Luke had just started receiving an allowance and was trying to save some money. "Oh, I don't know exactly," I answered. "First there's a monthly fee, and then there's a certain amount for daytime minutes and a different rate for evenings and weekends."

"You don't even know how much it costs?" Luke asked, twisting his lips into a crooked smirk.

"Well," I stammered, feeling a little foolish, "I think it costs about thirty cents a minute—peak hours, you know."

I tried to steer the conversation a different direction by pointing out the entrance to the park, but Luke was not about to drop the subject. "Well, how many minutes did we talk?"

"Probably five," I answered with just a trace of irritation in my voice.

There was a long silence while Luke counted on his fingers and muttered under his breath. Then he shook his head, wiped his brow, and said, "Grandma Gracie, don't you know you can make calls for five cents a minute and get cash back?"

Thankfully, we soon reached our destination and got out of the car. Using that strong right arm of mine, I directed my grandson to the playground. Then I plopped on a bench, called up my cellular provider, and asked about cheaper rates.

Unfortunately, Luke is not the only grandchild who has challenged my way of thinking. When his little brother Connor was four, the two boys were buckled in the backseat of my car as I drove the fifty miles from their house to ours. The further I drove, the more restless they became. Luke with his budding choleric personality asked a zillion questions, filling the spaces between my answers with uhhs and mmms so Connor couldn't get a word in edgewise. When he tried, Luke reminded him not to interrupt.

The situation seemed to me just another example of two tired, competitive kids vying for attention, but alas, I was due to learn yet another important life lesson from a most unlikely source—the insightful words of a preschooler.

Little Connor, the thoughtful young philosopher of the family, was not getting his share of my time, so he decided to create a break in the conversation by faking a sneeze. With a boisterous outburst of air, he let out two rather convincing attempts: "Achoo, *achoooo!*"

Luke was much too shrewd to be fooled by such antics. "You're faking!" he yelled at his little brother, then turning to me, duly reported, "That was not a real sneeze. Grandma Gracie, Connor's faking."

"Yes, it was a real sneeze," Connor insisted.

"Was not!" Luke shouted.

"Was too!'

"Was not!"

"Was too!"

After a few more rounds of this verbal tug-of-war, I intervened—loudly.

MY RESIGNATION FROM ADULTHOOD

Repeat this to yourself or with a friend: I am hereby officially tendering my resignation as an adult.

- **I have decided I would like to accept the responsibilities of an eight-year-old again.** I want to go to McDonald's and think that it's a four-star restaurant. I want to sail sticks across a fresh mud puddle and make ripples with rocks. I want to think M&M's are better than money because you can eat them. I want to lie under a big oak tree and run a lemonade stand with my friends on a hot summer's day.

- **I want to return to a time when life was innocent**—when the most important thing was to know colors, multiplication tables, and nursery rhymes; and when I didn't know what I didn't know . . . I didn't care. Remember that time when all you knew was to be happy because you were blissfully unaware of all the things that should make you worried or upset?

- **I want to think the world is fair,** and I want to believe, even without reason, that everyone is honest and good.

- **I want to believe that anything is possible**—oblivious to the complexities of life and overly excited by the little things again.

- **I want to live simple again.** I no longer want to allow my day to be overrun by computer crashes, mountains of paperwork, depressing news, how to survive more days in the month than there is money in the bank, doctor bills, gossip, illness, and loss. I want to believe in the power of smiles, hugs, a kind word, truth, justice, peace, dreams, the imagination, mankind, and making angels in the snow.

So . . . here's my checkbook and my car keys, my credit card bills, and my 401(k) statements. I am officially resigning from adulthood. And if you want to discuss this further, you'll have to catch me first, 'cause . . .

"Tag! You're it!"[2]

36

"Guys! How important is it? Really?"

A startled hush settled over the battling backseat duo. For the next few minutes, I was Queen Mother of a much quieter court. But all the while Connor was thinking over my rhetorical questions, working up his own answer.

Finally, in a voice brimming with confidence, he declared, "Everything's important 'bout me!"

This little boy's self-esteem did not depend on the attention (or lack of attention) he received, on his brother's approval or disapproval, or even on his grandmother's unintentional snubbing. Connor knew he was important, and nothing would convince him otherwise. Now, I ask you, how could anyone argue with logic like that?

I couldn't help but smile as I whispered a prayer on his behalf. "Lord, thank you for Connor's positive outlook on life. May he never lose that robust sense of self and healthy pride."

As we sped on down the highway, my thoughts turned to my other offspring—each with their own unique personalities and gifts. I thought about their fresh, uncluttered minds and their hearts so free and full of faith.

Through the years, my children and grandchildren have amazed me with their maturity and everyday common sense. They've helped me grow, showing me things I needed to change. And all the while they have loved me with unconditional love.

No wonder the Bible tells us, "A little child will lead them."

I just hope I won't become so old-fashioned or set in my ways that I cannot follow.

3

All I Really Need to Know I Learned from Girlfriends

CELEBRATING MIDLIFE FRIENDSHIPS

My friends have made the story of my life. In a thousand ways they have turned my limitations into beautiful privileges, and enabled me to walk serene and happy.

Helen Keller

As I settled into a pew near the front of the auditorium, I heard Linda's cheerful voice coming from the nearby aisle. "Hey there, girlfriend!"

I turned in the direction of the warm greeting and stood to give her a big Sunday-morning hug. Girlfriend. In the two years that I've known Linda, it's a term of endearment I've heard her use often, not only with me, but with dozens of other friends. Even though the term may be a bit overused today, the thought of having a real girlfriend warms my heart like a piping hot cinnamon roll on a winter morning. Especially since I'm still adjusting to life in the bustling Dallas–Fort Worth area after spending twenty-some years in the boondocks of East Texas.

When I told Linda how her greeting made me feel, she clued me in on some GF history. "Seems like everybody from the Ya-Ya Sisters to the Golden Girls calls each other girlfriend these days," Linda said, "but I may have been the one to start that trend." She went on to explain, "You know, I'm the mother of three girls, and even when they were little, I called them my girlfriends. When I wanted to take them shopping, I'd say, 'Come on, girlfriends, let's go to town.' They jumped into the car faster than giddy kangaroos—ready to fill their shopping pouches full."

As I listened, I imagined Linda dressed in a 1960s style housedress and crisp white apron—a June Cleaver look-alike—rounding up her pretty little girls and heading off to do the things that girls from six to sixty love to do together. Linda said the girls liked to go shopping or to the beauty shop or spend an afternoon at the swimming pool. Usually they'd wrap up their outing by having a picnic or doing lunch. It seems to me that Linda and her three daughters were (and still are for that matter) girlfriends in the truest sense of the word.

For me, being included in her circle of friends is a real honor, since the position is obviously reserved for folks she considers to be very special.

Before the church service got started, my mind relived a recent jaunt I'd taken with Linda and a whole gaggle of other gals—Shirley, Barbara, Betty, Madge, Joanne, and Edna. We had made big plans to celebrate Barbara's birthday in Salado, a quaint Texas town known for its crafts and antiques stores. We'd scarcely pulled out of Linda's driveway and into the mainstream of traffic when I realized these gals were destined to become great friends of mine. They were warm, funny, and most importantly, willing to make room in their well-established circle for a newcomer like me. By the time we pulled into the parking lot at Stagecoach Inn, we were laughing and carrying on as if we'd known each other for years.

For two days and nights, we shopped for antiques, jewelry, and objects of art; dined in Salado's finest eateries; and lounged in our rooms decked out in our pajamas and slippers. We laughed over silly stories, rejoiced about some of our children's successes, and when one gal revealed that her daughter was getting a divorce, shed a few tears. The next morning at breakfast, we giggled about who could snore loudest and who stayed up latest. Now that I think about it, our outing wasn't much different than the sleepovers I enjoyed as a teenager—thus proving the adage, you're never too old to enjoy a slumber party.

On the way home, we decided to stop in Hillsboro for a quick lunch. We missed the exit that would have taken us to a lovely sandwich shop, exited at the next ramp, circled through a parking lot, and somehow ended up back on the highway. Rather than retrace our steps (a task that could put a bunch of gals like us into a literal tailspin), we decided to stop at the next restaurant we spotted. As it turned out, we rounded a corner and saw a large café . . . on the right side of the road. The sign out front read, Lone Star Café—Bubba

Likes It! Now, I ask you, how could any well-bred group of Texas women resist a recommendation like that?

We whipped into the parking lot and herded inside, making a quick stop at the restrooms marked suitably Bubbas and Bubbettes. Leaving the Bubbettes' room, we located a table for eight and checked out the menu. Hmm . . . Bubba Burgers, Bubba Beans, Bubbalow Wings, and to drink, Bubbaritas. We loosened our belts and dined sumptuously on Big Bacon Bubba Burgers and Beans (opting for Diet Coke instead of Bubbaritas).

Back on the road, I rested my head on the backseat in Linda's Mercedes, and the words from a simple song I learned in Girl Scouts trekked through my brain. "Make new friends, but keep the old. One is silver and the other gold." I breathed a prayer, thanking God for the unique treasure that friends are. I thanked him for the "golden" friends—the gals I've kept

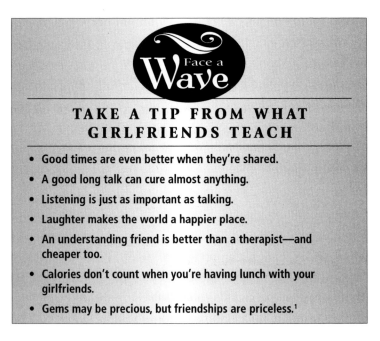

TAKE A TIP FROM WHAT GIRLFRIENDS TEACH

- Good times are even better when they're shared.
- A good long talk can cure almost anything.
- Listening is just as important as talking.
- Laughter makes the world a happier place.
- An understanding friend is better than a therapist—and cheaper too.
- Calories don't count when you're having lunch with your girlfriends.
- Gems may be precious, but friendships are priceless.[1]

in touch with for more than two decades, and I said thank you for these "silver" friends who had opened their arms and widened their circle to include me. I felt blessed indeed.

My mind focused on an email I'd recently received. The message claimed there are three categories of friends—some friends are for a season, some friends are for a reason, and still others are meant to last a lifetime.

As we sped down the highway, lush green pastures dotted with bluebonnets and Indian paintbrush flashed by my window, and since I was in a reflective mood, my thoughts turned toward the friendships I've enjoyed throughout my adult years. Some friends came into my life for a season. We loved each other, but after a while we went our separate ways. Some of my for-a-season friends moved to distant cities, and others developed interests that were very different from mine. Still, I look back on those friendships with a smile on my face, thankful for having been close for that special period of time.

Other friendships were for a reason. We worked on a mutual project at school or church, or we both taught Bible study groups. Some of my for-a-reason friends were soccer moms or carpool buddies. Others entered my circle, bringing their unique gifts and insights to enrich my life for a specific purpose. These friends provided closeness and camaraderie and shared mutual interests and ideas when they were needed most. Interestingly, when the reason to be together was gone, so was the friendship.

Other friendships have lasted a lifetime—at least so far, since my lifetime is not quite finished. I only have a few friends who fit into this category. These are the kindred spirits who rejoiced over the birth of my children and shed empathetic tears when they encountered life's inevitable suffering. They were with me during our birthday parties, graduations, weddings, and the births of my grandchildren. With these few, I share details of my life, my goals, and my spiritual pursuits, as well as my difficulties and sorrows. My "friends for a lifetime" know things about me that nobody else knows, and I can count on them to keep my confidences.

Seems to me it would be a mistake to consider every friend a potential lifetime bosom buddy or kindred spirit. In reality these are rare and precious. You just can't make intimacy happen. But when we relax and enjoy the company of others, we give God the opportunity to do something amazing if he sees fit. Sometimes friendships morph from one stage of development to another—from casual acquaintance to cherished confidant.

As I considered this group of friends who accompanied me in Linda's car, I just knew that some of them would be second-half-of-lifetime friends. A deep-seated feeling of contentment settled into my soul, as well as the feeling of being bone tired after three days of don't-stop-till-you-drop shopping.

Later that evening as I settled in my bed and pulled the soft comforter up to my chin, my thoughts again turned to the subject of friends and how vital they are. I had recently read that friends are good for a woman's health. They ease the stress in our lives, lift depression, and actually prevent illness. Besides that, we all know that friends are good for a woman's emotional and spiritual well-being. As we share personal issues with a friend who understands, she really does double our joy and divide our sorrow.

We may have come a long way since we stood around a campfire in our scout uniforms and, with the glowing embers casting a bright glow on our faces, sang, "Make new friends but keep the old." We've become a lot busier; our families, careers, and other interests have complicated our lives. But we never outgrow our need for friends. Maybe we need them even more in our second half of life.

As I drifted off to sleep, words from the pen of Solomon, the wise king of Israel, played about in my mind. "Two are better than one, because they have a good return for their work. If one falls down, his friend can help him up, but pity the man who falls and has no one to help him up! Also, if two lie down together, they will keep warm, but how can one keep warm alone? Though one may be overpowered, two can defend themselves. A cord of three strands is not quickly broken."[2] I woke the next morning feeling refreshed and happy.

A few weeks later I answered the phone and recognized the voice of another new friend, Annette. "Gracie, there's a group of four women planning a trip to Seattle, and, well . . . we voted, and it's unanimous. We want you to go along."

I felt my excitement level rising as I answered, "I'm so glad I made the cut. Of course I'll go!"

(The ability to make such spontaneous decisions is one reason why some gals consider the second half of life the best half. With diminished responsibilities at home and a little more financial freedom, well . . . why not take a trip with the girls?)

Before the week ended, five gals known for their spontaneity—Annette, Shirley, Pat, Peggy, and I—met (at a res-

make a
Splash

JUST FOR FUN!

Gather your girlfriends for these Top 10 games at girls-in-midlife parties:

1. Sag, You're It!
2. Pin the Toupee on the Bald Guy
3. 20 Questions Shouted into Your Good Ear
4. Kick the Bucket
5. Red Rover, Red Rover, the Nurse Says Bend Over
6. Doc, Doc, Goose
7. Simon Says Something Incoherent
8. Hide and Go Pee
9. Spin the Bottle of Mylanta
10. Musical Recliners

taurant of course) to discuss the details. Before the month's end, we gathered at the airport, clutching our tickets and dragging stuffed-to-the-brim luggage with both hands. Imagine five women who've adopted the when-I-am-old-I-shall-wear-purple philosophy, packing enough tourist garb to last seven days! We must have been a sight to behold as we trailed through airport security checkpoints.

Annette's son and daughter-in-law, Jay and Nancy, had invited us to stay in their condominium in the beautiful Cascade Mountains. They even graciously allowed us to use their minivan. When we arrived, Nancy met us at the airport to hand over the keys. Before midnight we had located the condo, lugged a dozen suitcases up three flights of stairs, and fussed over which bed each of us would occupy. Then we crashed and slept like babies, while Pat's sound machine, simulating ocean waves, droned in the background. The next morning as the sun peeked over the mountain, I smelled coffee and heard somebody rustling through cereal boxes. I stumbled toward the coffeepot, grunted at Annette, and sank into a chair at the table. Before long the kitchen was bustling with girlfriends foraging for food.

After breakfast we got dressed—in purple and scarlet, no less! But we'd no sooner gathered our purses and visors and started toward the door than we encountered our first problem. Actually, it was the only problem we'd face during the entire vacation, but it was an ongoing issue. Nobody could figure out what to do next! In this group of five women, all having equal leadership skills, not one rose to the surface as Tour Guide in Charge.

After several fits and starts, we finally boarded the minivan and drove to downtown Seattle to explore the nooks and crannies of Pike Place Market. We must have looked like a female version of the Three Stooges (make that Five Stooges) as we parked our car on a hill and stumbled toward the brass pig that marked the entrance. We were heading down the street, lined up like ducks in a row, when the gal up front spotted something special in a store window, did a U-turn, and took off in the opposite direction. The rest of us followed obediently. We lined up again, but another gal who'd worked her way to the forefront ducked into a charming little boutique. Before we could all follow her through the door, she changed her mind, whirled around, and headed back outside.

Unfortunately, things didn't improve once we pushed our way inside the famous farmer's market. We rambled around, bumping into each other all day long like Larry, Curly, and Moe while we picked through the fresh produce on the farm tables and examined local craftspeople's handmade gifts stacked in the market's highstalls. Still, in spite of being directionally challenged, we managed to purchase enough of the market's goods to make our arthritic backbones ache as we wandered around toting our packages. We were still trying to follow the leader—even though the status of the one trying to lead was in serious question—when we left the market to do lunch.

We finally located Etta's Café, a popular restaurant, settled into a booth, and dined on the best crab cakes and lemon meringue pie anybody could remember. (But with our questionable memories, "best" is a relative term!) After lunch we managed to hang together well enough to explore most of Seattle's seafront before we found our car and made the trip back to our "home" away from home. That evening we plowed through our goody bags and shared the booty. We snacked on fresh fruits, spiced nuts, Chukar cherries, English crumpets, chocolate candy, and enough Seattle's Best Coffee to float a battleship.

For the next few days, we cruised the streets of downtown, motored along the scenic roads that wind through the Cascades, and spent hours gazing at the mountains off the deck of our condo, relaxing in the crisp, cool air. One day we boarded a hydroplane and traveled over deep blue Pacific waters to Victoria, British Columbia, where we toured and shopped some more. We strolled through the beautiful Butchart Gardens and sipped tea at the Fairmont Empress Hotel.

By the time Sunday came around, Annette elbowed her way in as temporary leader, announcing a plan she'd been mulling over for several days. "I want to take you to my favorite spot on the map." She grinned and added, "Anybody going with me?" Since nobody wanted to be left out, we piled into the minivan. With Annette behind the wheel, we took a scenic drive over Snoqualmie Pass, turned onto a winding back road, and ended up in Roslyn. Our first stop was the famous Roslyn Café, setting of the once popular TV series *Northern Exposure*. (Apparently Roslyn in the winter could easily double for Cicely, Alaska.)

We checked out the ancient building with its rugged décor, then climbed onto the tall stools at the bar and ordered hamburgers and lemonade. Afterward we roamed up and down the quaint streets of Roslyn, peeking in the gift shops and left-behind movie sets, before heading up the mountain to Annette's favorite spot.

After a short drive, Annette pulled the minivan off the highway onto a dirt road and shut off the engine. As we climbed out, we heard the sound of rushing water. Eager to see what was on the other side of the tree line, we pushed through the undergrowth. We stepped into a clearing, and the view was breathtaking—clear, blue water churned over massive, gray boulders, and jagged, white-faced cliffs stood majestically on the other side. We tiptoed across an area of rocks that had been washed smooth and deposited on the rugged shore and watched the river tumble downstream toward Russell Lake.

For a while we wandered up and down the banks of the river, picking up a few smooth stones and pieces of driftwood, seeking a few moments of solitude. Annette sat down on a flat rock, stripped off her shoes and socks, and slipped her feet into the cold water. I managed to hoist myself onto the trunk of a huge fallen tree that had washed up on the rocky shore. There I sat in rapt silence, trying to take in the magnificent scene.

The sun beamed overhead, and I felt an overwhelming sense of God's presence. I sang softly, "Amazing grace, how sweet the sound. . . ."

Shirley climbed up beside me and sang alto, "I once was lost but now am found, was blind, but now I see. . . ."

Pat and Peggy joined in. Annette dried her feet on the bottom of her T-shirt, put on her shoes, and wandered over. Leaning against the tree and gazing up toward the cliffs, her face took on a heavenly glow, and I understood why this spot was her "favorite place on the map." I glanced at Peggy and caught her wiping tears on her sleeve. I wondered if she was thinking about her husband who'd recently passed away. In a clear soprano voice, she led out on the final stanza. "When we've been there ten thousand years, bright shining as the sun, we've no less days to sing God's praise than when we first begun." For at least half an hour we sang together, belting out our favorite hymns and choruses. Then the music gave way to silence.

Nobody spoke as we headed back to the minivan. The presence of God seemed to hover over us while we buckled our seat belts and pulled onto the mountain roadway. There was no doubt about it. Our motley crew had experienced a divine encounter. We'd worshiped that Sunday afternoon in a chapel of our own choosing with a gray weathered tree trunk as our pew. Our slightly off-key harmony bouncing off the rugged mountain wall could not have sounded more beautiful had it been reverberating off the near-perfect acoustics in our church sanctuary back home. Perhaps more than any other time in my life, I knew what it meant to praise our Creator.

For several miles we traveled quietly. Then Pat broke the silence—with another song, of all things. "I'll be down to get you in a taxi, honey. You better be ready about half past eight." The rest of us joined in, "Now, dearie, don't be late. I want to be there when the band starts playing. . . ." From there we launched into another classic. "Five-foot-two, eyes of blue, but oh, what those five-foot could do. Has anybody seen my gal?" By the time we got to the "could she, could she, could she coo" part of the song, we were swaying and laughing merrily. We sang, laughed, and told stories all the way "home."

When we reached our condo, we were in a state of near exhaustion from the afternoon's physical exertion, almost totally breathless from singing, and more than a little awestruck. But I think I can speak for all of us when I say our hearts were filled to the brim with love, joy, and peace.

As for me, my blessings were multiplied, because I'd shared them with an amazing group of really good friends. I hadn't known them long, but I could without hesitation call them my girlfriends. And without any reservation, I would also dub them the best travelin' Bubbettes I've ever tagged along with.

PART 2

Keeping Adventure
(and the Body) Alive

4

Over the Hill
and On a Roll

SAILING WITH EAGLES

Those who hope in the LORD
   will renew their strength.
They will soar on wings like eagles;
   they will run and not grow weary,
   they will walk and not be faint.
                              Isaiah 40:31

When I first met Annette at church, I thought, *Now there's a gal I want to know better!* She stood barely five feet tall, with a stylish wedge of blonde hair and blue eyes that twinkled mischievously. Decked out in a classy outfit of denim and lace, she looked quite the lady. But just beneath the soft, feminine exterior beat the heart of a strong woman—a gal who was athletic, maybe even a little bit tough. If she'd had a pair of ice skates slung over her shoulder that day, she'd have looked like a slightly older version of Dorothy Hamill.

I looked for Annette again the next Sunday and the next. It wasn't until two weeks later that she showed up at church again. I was thrilled. Even though we'd only met one time, we walked down the hall toward the auditorium jabbering excitedly like two lifelong friends. "Where in the world have you been?" I asked. "I've looked for you, wondered if you were out of town or something."

"Actually," she said, "I just got back from Seattle. I spent a few weeks with my kids and grandkids." Then a big grin crossed her face as she quickly added, "I went paragliding!"

"You did what?" I put my arm around her shoulders and noticed how she seemed to fit right underneath. I thought, *This gal may be tiny, but she's got a great, big, adventuresome soul.* "You mean you jumped off a mountain?" My eyes widened with the excitement of it all. "Were you scared? You've got to tell me all about it!"

A few weeks later we met for coffee, and she did just that.

We'd scarcely slid into a booth at Mimi's Café when Annette began, "Oh, Gracie, it was just like flying. At one point, I looked down and saw an eagle soaring through the sky beneath us."

"Us?" I interrupted, as I'm sometimes prone to do when I can't wait to get to the juicy part of the story. "You didn't jump by yourself?"

"Hey, I may be reckless, but I'm not crazy!" Annette took a sip of coffee. "I jumped in tandem with an experienced glider named Marc. We were strapped into a harness together like two old mules."

I stirred a splash of cream into my coffee, settled into the soft booth, and waited for Annette to back up and start from the beginning.

Seems even as a child Annette had wanted to fly. Sometimes she would tie a towel around her neck and run around the yard as fast as she could go, hoping to take off into the wild blue yonder like Superwoman. Later, as a daring pre-adolescent, she would climb on top of the barn and jump off. When she got older, she wanted to try her wings at sky-diving. She thought about it often and was determined to follow her heart. She vowed that before she died, she would parachute out of a plane! But years passed and her dream had not become a reality.

Then one summer while visiting Seattle, she noticed the paragliders, with their purple, green, and fuchsia wings, sailing like giant birds around the jagged rocks and cliffs of Tiger Mountain. Her lifelong dream to fly, always glowing like an ember just beneath the surface of her heart, was fanned into a red-hot flame.

Sometimes she would park her car at the foot of the mountain and watch the gliders make their final swoops back and forth above the tops of the evergreen trees, then come in for a landing in the grassy meadow. As she watched, she thought, *I could do that!*

One morning Annette and her daughter-in-law, Nancy, sat on the futon in Nancy's outdoor living area and sipped their morning coffee. As the ceiling fan whirred above their heads, Annette picked up a conversation that had begun the day before. "Oh, Nancy, it would be such fun to sail around that mountain."

"You're serious!" Nancy said. "You really want to do this, don't you?"

"I will do it, someday," Annette declared, "and I want you and Jay and the boys to be there, watching."

Later that morning Nancy decided to help her mother-in-law follow her heart. She called Marc Chirico, the owner of Go Sky High, the local paragliding club, to gather some information. "For some crazy reason, my mother-in-law wants to jump off Tiger Mountain," Nancy said. "Can you teach her how to do it? And, by the way, how much does it cost?"

A lively voice on the other end of the line answered, "I can teach anybody how to fly, and as far as the cost is concerned, well, how much do you like your mother-in-law?"

Nancy assured the guy she was quite fond of Annette and not in the market for a mother-in-law hit man. With that fact clearly established, Nancy had a couple of other questions. "My mother-in-law has high blood pressure, but she takes medication. Is that a problem?"

"Nope!" Marc answered confidently. "No problem."

"I guess I ought to tell you, she's had two bypass operations on her heart. Do you still think she'll be okay?" Before he could answer, just to be on the safe side, Nancy added, "And, well, my mother-in-law is no spring chicken, if you know what I mean."

"Lady, I've taken old people up on that mountain in a wheelchair," Marc said. "She'll be just fine."

The next day Annette paid the fee, signed a release, and scheduled a time to leap.

A few days later at the appointed time, Nancy and Annette pulled into the parking lot at the foot of the mountain and approached the man who appeared to be in charge. When Nancy introduced herself, Marc shook her hand, looked at Annette, then with a puzzled expression on his face asked, "Where's the victim?" Seems the pint-sized lady wearing jeans, a denim jacket, hiking boots, and her bright blue sweatshirt printed with kitty cats was not exactly what the guy had expected.

Nancy reached for Annette's hand and declared, "This is my mother-in-law."

"Heck," Marc said, "I thought I was taking up an old lady. Why, this'll be a piece o' cake." Then he winked at Annette and asked, "By the way, are you married?"

Marc looked to be in his thirties, a seasoned outdoorsman, wearing rugged jeans, a denim shirt, and a navy cap. If Annette had any apprehension at all, it vanished after meeting him. The guy seemed confident, and besides that, he made her laugh.

Marc grinned and said, "Let's practice!" He helped Annette into a harness, tightened the belts, and strapped her in a leather seat suspended from a wooden frame. "Now," he began, "jump up and down a few times to get the feel of it."

Annette got "the feel" all right. She felt like a baby in a Johnny Jump-up hung from a kitchen doorway. As she hopped around on her toes, she wondered if this was what folks meant when they talked about being in their second childhood.

After the brief lesson, Annette and eight other jumpers climbed in the back of Marc's truck while he loaded the wings on top. Annette braced herself as the old truck sputtered, then groaned and lurched its way upward. For almost an hour they traversed the face of the mountain on steep logging trails. She felt every bump on the narrow road pitted with chuckholes and deep ruts.

When they reached the mountaintop and parked, Annette jumped off the truck eager to explore the launching site. The first thing she spotted was a cedar carving of a crouched tiger. From the toes of its outstretched paws to the tip of its tail, the crude work of art measured at least ten feet. The tiger had wings, like the wings of an eagle, folded on each side. As Annette gazed at the primitive sculpture, her heart filled with joy. To her it represented the lionhearted effort required to run and jump, the inner strength she needed to take that leap, and the wings necessary to make her dreams come true.

She walked to the launching area where a crude contraption called "the rack" had been constructed. Marc explained, "Each jumper stands beneath the rack while their wings are attached to the leather harness. After the equipment has been checked, they step forward, leaving the rack behind, and begin their running start toward the precipice of the mountain." Marc told Annette it would take about twenty steps to get from the rack to "lift off."

At this point in the story, Annette motioned to the waitress and asked for a refill of decaffeinated coffee. I asked for a refill too—but not of decaf. Before I could listen to more, I needed another jolt of the real thing. Annette took a sip of the warm brew and said, "Gracie, standing there, looking at that contraption, then glancing toward the edge of the mountain, I felt my first bit of concern."

"Oh, Annette, I know you just had to be scared silly!" I said as I searched her eyes for just one tiny little sign that she needed a touch of sympathy.

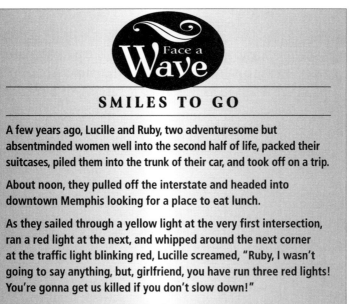

SMILES TO GO

A few years ago, Lucille and Ruby, two adventuresome but absentminded women well into the second half of life, packed their suitcases, piled them into the trunk of their car, and took off on a trip.

About noon, they pulled off the interstate and headed into downtown Memphis looking for a place to eat lunch.

As they sailed through a yellow light at the very first intersection, ran a red light at the next, and whipped around the next corner at the traffic light blinking red, Lucille screamed, "Ruby, I wasn't going to say anything, but, girlfriend, you have run three red lights! You're gonna get us killed if you don't slow down!"

With that, Ruby slapped her hand on her forehead and hollered, "Oh my gosh! Am I driving?"

"What are you talking about?" Annette giggled. "I wasn't scared. I just didn't know if I could run twenty steps without losing my breath!"

At that, we burst into laughter. Once she regained her composure, Annette said, "For practice, I ran as fast as I could go toward the edge of the mountain. When I got close to the edge, I threw on my brakes. After I knew I could run, I was ready to take the plunge!"

"Don't tell me you weren't frightened, just a little bit!" I persisted.

"Gracie," Annette grinned and said, "I can honestly say I never felt anything but excitement. I had decided beforehand, if I felt even a moment of fear, I wouldn't jump. Feeling anxious wouldn't be good for my heart. But I wasn't afraid, not at all."

Shortly after her trial run, it was Annette's turn to jump. She took her place on the rack, and Marc fastened her harness to the wings. Then he hooked up behind her. They moved forward in the rack until their feet were firmly planted on the ground. As the cool mountain air whistled around them, Marc yelled into Annette's ear, "When I say go, run straight toward the edge. Count the steps out loud so we can stay together. And don't do the 'mule step' on me. If you balk, I'll fall on top of you, and we'll both tumble over the edge."

Annette breathed a quick prayer and, with eyes wide open, started running as fast as her short little legs could go, straight toward the edge of the mountain. Marc was at her heels, running in sync. "One," she shouted, "two . . . seventeen, eighteen, nineteen, twenty, twenty-onnnne—" Air filled the wings; Annette's feet left the ground, and suddenly she was an eagle soaring in the crisp mountain air. Riding the wind.

"Take the handles," Marc yelled. "Pull the right one to go this way, the left to circle back around." Then he added this caution: "Remember, if you pull both the handles down, the air goes out of the sails."

Annette nodded, and she pulled the right handle and the craft headed north, sailing near the jagged rocks and cliffs of the northern face. In the distance she could see the Seattle skyline silhouetted against the bright blue sky. She tugged on the left handle and sailed southward over the emerald green peaks. On the horizon she caught a glimpse of Mount Baker, one of the highest summits in the Cascades. The clear blue water of Lake Sammamish glistened in the plains below.

Annette tugged on the handles again, and as she sailed past the northern cliffs, she spotted the eagle. It was soaring nearby, its wings outspread, white-tipped feathers fluttering in the breeze. Annette wanted to follow the majestic creature but realized her man-made nylon wings were no match for the real thing. The eagle dipped and disappeared from view.

Marc yelled, "She's trying to lead us away from her nest. She must have baby eaglets tucked away in one of those crevices."

Annette made another pass and was sailing into the sunset. The sky was painted with bright, buttery yellow streaks. Annette felt as though she were looking into the very face of God as she turned her wings and headed south again. The mountains and hills took on a mystical glow, and the words of a familiar psalm burned in her heart: "The heavens declare the glory of God; the skies proclaim the work of his hands."[1]

About forty-five minutes after she'd taken the plunge off Tiger Mountain, Annette began losing altitude. She made one final pass over the blackberry bushes near the foothills. Then it was time to prepare for a landing. She scooted forward in her seat, then pushed the leather swing out of the way behind her. For the last few minutes of the ride, she hung suspended only by the belt of the harness.

"Annette, how could you do that?" I cringed at the thought of it. "That would positively scare the bejeebers out of me!"

"Oh, Gracie," Annette giggled. "That was the best part of the ride! When I pushed myself out of that seat, I felt completely free, as free as a bird. You know how I've always wanted to parachute from an airplane. Well, when only the belts were fastened around me, I thought, this is just like parachuting from a plane. Maybe even better!"

I shook my head in disbelief as Annette took a deep breath and said, "I pulled downward on the handles, slowly allowing the air to escape from under the wings. Marc shouted in my ear, 'Now, remember, when we land, don't plant your feet. Run!'" Annette grinned and added, "I got my feet and legs a-going, running in place while I was still fifty feet in the air."

Her family and friends were waiting in the open field, their cameras clicking wildly when Annette came down. Her feet and legs were churning like a windmill. But when her boots touched the turf, Annette nailed her landing like a gymnast coming off the parallel bars.

She fell flat on her face. Marc landed on top of her, and the wings collapsed in a crumpled heap. Of course she realized immediately what she'd done. She started giggling and laughing out loud, realizing she looked like a housefly caught in a spiderweb. Annette laughed so hard that she cried, as Marc struggled to climb off her backside and out from under the scrunched-up wings. And while Marc was trying to free himself from the tangled mess, Annette had struggles of her own going on. She pushed aside the bundle of purple nylon and found herself nose to nose with a huge slobbering German shepherd. Apparently the dog thought Annette landed in his meadow for the sole purpose of playing with him.

To her continuing surprise, Annette soon found herself surrounded by people trying to help—the dog's owner, Jay and Nancy, her grandchildren Charlie and Cody, and Marc. Seeing her tears, they voiced a chorus of concern: "Annette, are you hurt?" "Nonnie, are you alright?" "Ma'am, you okay?"

Annette scrambled to her feet and faced the clamoring crowd. With her hands firmly planted on her hips, she gave them a look that stopped them all midsentence. An expectant hush settled over the group as she wiped the sticky mixture

CHOOSE WHAT REALLY MATTERS

An eighty-three-year-old woman's letter to a friend is like a wake-up call to us. Consider her heart:

I'm reading more and dusting less. I'm sitting in the yard and admiring the view without fussing about the weeds in the garden. I'm spending more time with my family and friends and less time working.

Whenever possible, life should be a pattern of experiences to savor not to endure. I'm trying to recognize these moments now and cherish them. I'm not "saving" anything; we use our good china and crystal for every special event such as losing a pound, getting the sink unstopped, or the first amaryllis blossom. I wear my good blazer to the market. My theory is if I look prosperous, I can shell out $28.49 for one small bag of groceries.

I'm not saving my good perfume for special parties but wearing it for clerks in the hardware store and tellers at the bank. "Someday" and "one of these days" are losing their grip on my vocabulary. If it's worth seeing or hearing or doing, I want to see and hear and do it *now*.

I'm not sure what others would've done had they known that they wouldn't be here for the tomorrow that we all take for granted. I think they would have called family members and a few close friends. They might have called a few former friends to apologize and mend fences for past squabbles. I like to think they would have gone out for a Chinese dinner, or for whatever their favorite food was. I'm guessing; I'll never know. It's those little things left undone that would make me angry if I knew my hours were limited. Angry because I hadn't written certain letters that I intended to write one of these days. Angry and sorry that I didn't tell my husband and parents often enough how much I truly love them. I'm trying very hard not to put off, hold back, or save anything that would add laughter and luster to our lives. And every morning when I open my eyes, I tell myself that it is special. Every day, every minute, every breath truly is a gift from God.[2]

of doggy drool and happy tears from her cheeks with the sleeve of her jean jacket.

"What do you mean, am I okay?" she said. "I'm better than okay! The ride was fantastic. I'm not crying; I'm laughing."

Then, as she embraced her family in a group hug, she added, "How could I be anything else but absolutely great when my lifelong dream has just come true?"

My friend, what dreams do you have waiting to be fulfilled? What do you really want to do with the second half of your life? No matter what mountain you might face in the future, no matter how outlandish your dreams or far-reaching your goals, no matter what your age or physical limitations—it's never too late to start soaring.

So step out of the deep ruts on the Road Most Traveled, take a handful of Extra Strength Excedrin, and slip on your most comfy sneakers (or leather hiking boots). Then meet me at the airport. I'm going to Disneyland!

5

Archaeologists Know the Best Dirt

❧

FOLLOWING YOUR DREAMS

Life is either a daring adventure or nothing.
To keep our faces toward change and behave like free spirits
in the presence of fate is strength undefeatable.

Helen Keller

On Christmas morning as Brenda ripped the ribbons and wrapping from her last gift, she noticed the mischievous look on her hubby's face. *What's he up to?* she wondered. She popped the lid off the box. Tucked inside the crumpled tissue, she discovered a miniature shovel and pick along with a note: "Brenda, you'll need a shovel and a pick when you 'dig' in June."

A few days later, Brenda cornered me in the hall at church and whispered, "You'll never guess what I got for Christmas."

She was right! Later when we met for lunch, she filled me in on the details. As she talked, I found myself fingering the pearls my husband, Joe, had given me and wondered, *Would I trade these?* Probably not! But I had to admit, I'd never seen Brenda so effusive.

"I felt a rush of conflicting emotions," she said as she placed a napkin in her lap and took a sip of tea. "First of all," Brenda said, "I was thrilled. My desire to participate in an archaeological dig is a dream I've had for many years. But I also felt a wave of sadness, because Larry couldn't accompany me. We'd always talked about going together—someday. But Larry's staff position at church didn't include four weeks away in a foreign country.

"Also, Larry and I are expecting our first grandchild in February." Brenda rearranged the flatware on the table and muttered, "Gracie, what if the baby doesn't recognize me when I get back home?" She paused, then added, "And what if Laura needs a bit of advice or help, and I'm a gazillion miles away, completely out of cell phone range?"

I grinned as I reached across the table and patted her hand. "It'll be okay!"

Brenda took a deep breath and continued with her story.

Shortly after Christmas, Larry and Brenda had thoroughly discussed the upcoming trip, including reasons why the timing was perfect. For several years before moving to Grapevine, they had lived in Waco where they became friends with Dr. Bruce Cresson, a Baylor University professor who frequently spoke at their church. Brenda and Larry were both intrigued when they listened to him tell of his annual trip to Israel to excavate archaeological dig sites. But with their young

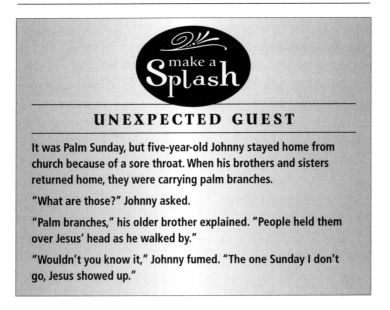

UNEXPECTED GUEST

It was Palm Sunday, but five-year-old Johnny stayed home from church because of a sore throat. When his brothers and sisters returned home, they were carrying palm branches.

"What are those?" Johnny asked.

"Palm branches," his older brother explained. "People held them over Jesus' head as he walked by."

"Wouldn't you know it," Johnny fumed. "The one Sunday I don't go, Jesus showed up."

daughters, Laura and Julie, at home plus the trip expenses, their dream vacation remained just that—a dream.

The couple tried to satisfy their hunger for adventure by taking a group on a typical tourist trip to Israel, then two years later they took a two-week trip to Jordan and Egypt. These excursions did not suffice. They were not content to simply "walk where Jesus walked"; they wanted to get their hands dirty—to sift through the soil where he actually lived.

Now I have to admit that my friend's desire to dig in two-thousand-year-old dirt is an enigma to me—a woman whose idea of roughing it means a hotel without a heated pool. Sometimes I wonder if Brenda's childhood experience lacked a few important elements. Perhaps she didn't get to make mud pies or build castles in the sand as I did growing up. At any rate, Brenda was determined. "Before I get old as dirt myself, I will go!"

However, when they discovered that Bruce would take his last Baylor excavation trip to the Holy Land prior to his retirement, Larry and Brenda knew this meant that "someday" had become "now or never." As they talked about the opportunity, Brenda realized what a special act of love Larry's Christmas gift conveyed. So she put aside her mixed feelings and began preparations for the trip of a lifetime.

Brenda and I finished our lunch, walked outside the café into the cold January air, and gave each other a big hug. It would be several months before I'd get to hear the rest of the story.

The next time we met for lunch, Brenda brought a box of artifacts she had purchased and a huge scrapbook documenting her trip. She took up the story where she'd previously left off.

"Gracie, one of the first things I did was call Linda, my friend for more years than either of us cares to admit. She lives out of state but was planning to go on the same trip! Throughout the spring we corresponded, mailing each other small gifts and cards. Most of the items we exchanged were completely useless—gardening knee pads, a tiny pocketknife—but all added to our excitement. I was glad to have a girlfriend to share the experience with."

Linda had flown into Dallas the day before the group was to depart. That evening, the two gals gathered a group of close-knit friends and did what most red-blooded Texas women do when dealing with frazzled emotions, like separation anxiety—they went out to eat Mexican food.

The next morning, a group of sixteen archaeologists and wannabes, ranging in age from twenty to seventy-something, gathered at the airport. According to Brenda, it was a diverse group—a few friends from Waco, several Baylor students participating for academic credit, and some complete strangers.

Even before they boarded the plane, the group was beginning to gel, and the fun had begun. As they waited, Brenda passed around a Waco newspaper that contained an article about a previous dig. A young man described the trip as "twenty days of the closest thing to hell that you can know." Jim, a man seated near Brenda, read those words out loud and shouted, "And . . . why haven't we seen this before?" Other team members burst out laughing, but at least with some, the hilarity seemed a bit forced.

Brenda's daughter, Laura; son-in-law, Greg; four-month-old grandson, Garrison; along with her husband, Larry, had come to see her off. (Her daughter, Julie, a flight attendant, was flying that day.) "Of course it was hard to say good-bye!" Brenda said. "But we'd no sooner settled in our seats than the sadness disappeared." Linda and Brenda talked and dozed and talked some more for the entire twenty-eight-hour trip. The level of excitement continued to build until, by the time they arrived in Tel Aviv, they were certain their hands would unearth the find of the millennium. Indiana Jones, move over!

After a two-hour drive to Arad, the group moved their belongings into a modest hotel, which would be their "home" for the next twenty-eight days. According to Brenda, the tiny room she and Linda would occupy was just a place to sleep, clean up, and wash their dirty clothes. The hotel's kitchen was kosher and the menu always good—although at times the food was a bit too interesting. Among the identifiable items, there were always bread, tomatoes, and cucumbers. The only place to get a soft drink was in the bar. Late-night jaunts to the bar proved to be an adventure for these two Baptist women, providing fodder for many funny stories and girlfriend giggles.

During the month-long excursion, Brenda and Linda did everything together—seatmates, roommates, dig partners, and nocturnal mischief-makers—and they were still friends when they got back home! Brenda said, "I think our girlfriends in Texas were praying for us! Really, I was so thankful for Linda. She definitely kept me from getting homesick."

The truth was they didn't have time to be homesick. Their daily schedule was grueling—a fact, at least according to the college students, that was not mentioned in the brochures advertising the trip. They were up at 4:00 a.m., ate a serve-yourself breakfast of bread and coffee in the deserted hotel dining room, then piled on the bus for a thirty-minute thrill-a-minute ride to the excavation site. By 5:30 they were climbing the hill of Tel Malhata. They worked hard until their midmorning break for a "real breakfast" provided by the hotel, stopped for a juice break at eleven, and ended their day's work at 1:00, before the heat became intolerable.

"Breakfast was so much fun!" Brenda said. "It was one of those times that proved that laughter is good medicine. We truly bonded and learned to love each other more as we laughed together." Brenda giggled while she recalled some of the congenial breakfasts they had shared in the shade of their makeshift tent. "All of us at one time or another managed to be entertained or became the entertainment because of someone's practical joke. Mostly we just enjoyed each other's foibles and missteps. One morning as one of the gals was scraping the bottom of a plastic container with her spoon, she was going on and on about the wonderful, yummy Israeli yogurt, when one of the college students announced, 'But . . . that's not yogurt; it's sour cream!' We laughed that day until the tears ran down our dust-covered cheeks, leaving little trails on our dirty faces."

Team members not only learned about the country's unique dairy products but learned a few important facts about Tel Malhata as well. The dig site was located in the Negev Desert about halfway between Arad and Beersheba. More than three thousand years ago, during the Iron Age, Tel Malhata was the site of a major city in the kingdom of Judah. Centuries before, a Hellenistic city had thrived there, and about the time of Jesus, a stonewalled Roman fortress stood on the same hill. Several hundred years after that, the site became a Bedouin burial ground. When Brenda first saw the tel, she noticed a Bedouin sheik's tomb on top—a vivid reminder that this had been their sacred land. Kaliel, a man from a nearby Bedouin camp, accompanied the archaeological team most days to make sure they did not disturb any of the graves.

"Not only was the schedule somewhat different than we had imagined, but so was the work!" Brenda grinned before launching into a detailed account of their mission. "We were each assigned a square in which to work under one of the supervisors. Linda and I were assigned to Dr. Alton Hassell, from Baylor's chemistry department. Our square was approximately fifteen feet by fifteen feet, and our instructions were to 'take it down like an elevator.' In other words, using our *teria* (a short-handled hoe), *patiche* (a small hand pick), trowel, and brush, we were to remove the dirt little by little, keeping the floor of the pit level as we did so. We hauled enough dirt to fill a dump truck—one bucketful at a time. It was the hardest, dirtiest work I'd ever done, but it was also the most rewarding. We took our floor down at least fifteen feet! We found lots of things, including a cooking installation, animal bones, oil lamps, bowls, a bead perhaps used as jewelry, bone spatulas, loom weights—items one would have used in a home at that time. We were touching things no human had touched since the Iron Age II, more than twenty-six hundred years ago!"

While the team worked, they could hear camels and donkeys braying in the fields nearby. As she listened, Brenda felt connected to the ancient people who had dwelled in the homes they were now exploring. She found herself wondering how a woman of that day might feel as she worked in the crowded space. Did she actually bake bread in the tiny brick oven? Were the bones left from one of their meals or carelessly dropped on the floor? How did she keep house? How would she have used or worn the items they were finding?

"Unearthing these treasures was an awesome experience and became an almost addictive search," Brenda said. "When we found something, feelings of euphoria were almost overwhelming. It was also humbling to compare the modest possessions we were uncovering to our lavish homes and all the possessions we need today." Brenda took a deep breath and, with a pensive look on her face, continued, "In that dirty, dusty, tiny pit, we never ran out of things to talk about. At times our conversations focused on our eternal God and his sustaining presence and provision throughout the ages. He was the factor that united their culture with ours. We talked about how the words of Scripture, penned in ancient times, still held true, providing inspiration for God's people today."

Brenda described the desert as "hot, dry, and windy, yet it was a beautiful place with breathtaking sunrises." Many mornings were shrouded in fog, but one morning in particular, as Brenda stood on the hill, the fog lifted just as the sun popped up over the crest of the tel. "My eyes filled with tears. I was awestruck by the reality of God's presence," she said. "I can only describe my feelings as deep gratitude—thankfulness to God for the heart-stopping beauty, the quietness, the opportunity of being in such a historic place. I felt completely overwhelmed."

Each afternoon, after returning to the hotel, Brenda and Linda would place their daily "finds" (mostly broken pieces of pottery) in a bucket of water to soak, then head to the hotel dining room for lunch, dirty clothes and all. After lunch they'd go back to their room to clean up. Linda would usually sink into a bathtub of warm water and Woolite with her dig clothes on—thus accomplishing two dirty jobs at one time. As soon as she cleaned out the tub, Brenda jumped in, choosing to shower while tromping her dirty garments underfoot. (Picture Lucy and Ethel stomping grapes!) Not only had these girls taken a step back in time, but they'd taken multitasking to a prehistoric level!

Afternoons were spent resting until time for pottery washing. "We scrubbed the previous day's finds with fingernail brushes and let them dry for twenty-four hours," Brenda explained. "Then the supervisors checked each piece to determine whether or not it would go to 'restoration' at Tel Aviv University or be tossed as unimportant. Hearing one of our personal finds declared good enough to go to 'restoration' became the highlight and reward of our day." Brenda couldn't wait to tell me about one of her important contributions to the university repository. It was a bone spatula—one of the largest and most complete found at Tel Malhata.

About once a week, Brenda and Linda would join the college students for a jaunt into town. "We shopped for vital necessities—like peanut butter!" Brenda grinned and added, "We'd feast on pizza, hamburgers—anything but cucumbers!"

On weekends the entire group piled into a small bus and traveled around Israel with Bruce as their guide. First stop on the tour was usually a place that served ice cream. "We developed a new appreciation for two American entrepreneurs, Ben and Jerry. We thanked God for dairy products we could recognize, and we loved Bruce for being so thoughtful!" Brenda's eyes twinkled as she told of their weekend excursions. "We saw all the typical tourist sites—Jerusalem, Jericho, Masada. Even though I had seen most of the places on a previous trip to Israel, I found myself looking at them differently and hearing new information because of what we were doing at the dig site. Our discoveries gave color and meaning to the familiar stories of the Bible." Brenda grinned mischievously. "Being the seasoned 'archaeologists' that we were, we couldn't help but feel a bit smug when we overheard the 'tourists' talk.

"Once while riding a bus from the hotel to the Old City in Jerusalem, we listened to a group talk about their 'dig for a day.' They were elated to have found a Roman coin! We looked at each other and rolled our eyes. A Roman coin, huh?" Brenda brushed her fingernails on her shirt and said, "Why, those only dated AD 100, and we, well, we were uncovering finds dated about 600 BC!"

Two weekends included overnight stays in Jerusalem, where the group observed the fascinating traditions and lifestyles of the many diverse peoples. Dr. Lynn Tatum, of Baylor's religion department, led five of them on a journey to experience Shabbat in the Meashearim, the Jewish orthodox section of Jerusalem. They were given instructions on how to dress and act (well covered, no clowning around) as they walked through the area following behind the two men in the group.

"We observed, up close and personal, how the people celebrated their Sabbath," Brenda explained. "It seemed sad to see how their lives were defined by so many laws. And I was thankful for Jesus' liberating act of love for us who believe. He truly did come that we might have life and the freedom to experience it more abundantly!" They followed Lynn through the Old City and other parts of Jerusalem, and everywhere the group went, he taught them the history, politics, and culture of Israel and its peoples. The little band returned to their hotel four hours after they started their journey, worn out from all the walking but thrilled at the things they had seen and heard. "I was so thankful for Lynn's willingness to teach us during those trips," Brenda said.

On another excursion into Jerusalem, the group toured the tunnels tracing the outer edge of the Temple Mount. As the crowd pressed around them, pushing their way into the area, Brenda experienced at least some of the passion and tension that permeates that land today. Later they observed faithful Jews tucking their scribbled prayers into the crevices of the Wailing Wall.

Their last weekend included a visit to Tel Aviv University and the restoration rooms, where they were able to see pieces of pottery similar to those they'd unearthed being put back together like a jigsaw puzzle. "It was truly a rare privilege to visit these rooms. The experience put the trip together for me," Brenda explained. "Seeing the restoration process helped me understand the importance of separating our finds by level and location. It made me proud to be part of such important discoveries."

According to Brenda, one of the most precious moments occurred near the end of her trip beside the Sea of Galilee. "We were staying at the Nof Ginosar Kibbutz on the western shore. On Sunday, Linda and I got up early and walked down to the beach. The sun was just rising over the Golan Heights on the eastern shore, and the sea was like glass. Except for the gentle lapping of water at the shoreline, there wasn't a sound to be heard. My mind transported me back to the time when Jesus walked on these very shores, and I envisioned him feeding more than five thousand with just a few tiny fish and loaves of bread. My mind's eye saw him cook fish over an open fire and feed his disciples. I relived the moment that Peter stepped out of his boat and walked toward his Lord—on these very waters. I opened my Bible and read what Jesus said to his impetuous disciple: 'Take courage! It is I. Don't be afraid.'[1]

"It seemed like a dream to be sitting in such a picturesque place, reading my Savior's own words. I picked up a handful of sand, allowed the grains to sift through my fingers, and relived the drama that had taken place on this shore. As I sat with my head bowed, I heard a soft buzzing sound coming from somewhere in the distance. Then it became louder and louder. I looked up and saw two Jet Skis going lickety-split through the placid water, leaving a white-tipped wake and making waves slap against the rocks nearby. I laughed . . . hard, as my thoughts were quickly transported back into the twenty-first century. Israel is definitely a mix of old and new. Then my thoughts turned toward home. I couldn't wait to see my family—especially my grandbaby, Garrison."

A few days later, Brenda, along with the rest of the crew, climbed aboard the plane for the long trip home. The feelings of euphoria they had experienced on the way over had now been replaced by deeply felt sentiment. "As I settled into my seat next to Linda, the events of the past month played through my mind like a video on fast forward," Brenda recalled. "As I revisited every day, relived each experience, I thanked God for Larry's sacrificial gift. I couldn't help but think about how much it had cost him both personally, being willing to go it alone for four weeks, and monetarily—that trip was expensive! A broad smile crossed my face as I made a mental list of what I 'got for my money.'

"I got to get dirtier than I'd ever been in my life! I got to haul a ton of dirt, one bucketful at a time. I got to be so tired I could hardly move my body from one place to another. And . . . I got to find and touch things that had not been seen or felt in over two thousand years. Besides that, I'd had

LIFE IN AMERICA CAN BE COMPLICATED

1. Only in America can a pizza get to your house faster than an ambulance.

2. Only in America are there handicap parking places in front of a skating rink.

3. Only in America do drugstores make the sick walk all the way to the back of the store to get their prescriptions while healthy people can buy cigarettes at the front.

4. Only in America do people order double cheeseburgers, large fries, and a Diet Coke.

5. Only in America do banks leave both doors open and then chain the pens to the counters.

6. Only in America do we leave cars worth thousands of dollars in the driveway and put our useless junk in the garage.

7. Only in America do we use answering machines to screen calls and then have call waiting so we won't miss a call from someone we didn't want to talk to in the first place.

8. Only in America do we buy hot dogs in packages of ten and buns in packages of eight.

9. Only in America do we use the word *politics* to describe the process so well. *Poli* in Latin means *many*, and *tics* means *bloodsucking creatures.*

10. Only in America do they have drive-up ATM machines with Braille lettering.[2]

more fun than ought to be legal. I had begun this trip clean, energetic, and excited; I'd ended it dirty and exhausted. But deep in my soul, in that place where God connects with the human spirit, I knew that I had been part of something really big! I also knew that I'd be heading home soon, back to my usual routine, but I would never be the same again. How could anything ever be the same, now that I'm a real archaeologist?"

For several days after talking to Brenda, my thoughts returned to her story again and again. I felt a real connection to my adventuresome friend and wished I could have been there in Israel with her instead of experiencing the journey secondhand. I also thought about the spiritual implications of the trip. In a flash of insight, I thought about how Brenda's adventure was a picture of spiritual journeys that all of us take at one time or another. God digs deep into the soil of our lives, where he does an excavation of our hearts. He locates the broken fragments, helps us identify them, then takes us to his restoration room where he delights in putting us back together to make a complete, perfect treasure. I guess you could say that God, our heavenly Father, is an archaeologist too.

6

Well-Aged Wisdom

Discovering the Value of Mentoring

> Have you ever noticed the difference in the Christian life between work and fruit? A machine can do work; only life can bear fruit.
>
> Andrew Murray

As a young Christian, my spiritual roots were planted deep in the soil of Southern Baptist fundamentalism. I knew right from wrong—at least concerning the clear-cut, black and white issues. But as I grew up, I discovered much about the Christian life that's gray, some matters of truth not easily defined and some just downright confusing. For example, I'd been taught that a person is saved to serve. So early on, I began looking for ways to serve God. Before long I was completely overwhelmed as I learned firsthand "the harvest is plentiful, but the workers are few."[1]

Because Jesus had done so much for me, I figured I should do whatever I could for him, as a sort of payback gesture. I jumped into the churning waters of Christian service with no water wings, and I didn't have a clue how to get back to shore once I had drifted into, well . . . some rather swift currents.

I wanted every child in the whole wide world to know about Jesus—well, at least every child in my hometown—and so I volunteered to teach Vacation Bible School. When the choir director heard I was a hard worker (believe me, this kind of news travels fast in Christendom!) he asked me to help with the children's choir, even though I had no musical talent. Later I joined the women's missionary society—how could I not join since I believed in international missions? Then I realized that my Sunday school teacher could use some help, so I volunteered to make phone calls, plan parties, and visit shut-ins. (This was something I enjoyed doing, so why not?) When they needed assistance in the church office, I showed up to fold bulletins, make copies, and sort envelopes. Why, I'd have swept the halls or polished pews into the sanctuary if anybody had asked.

After a few years of this kind of feverish activity, I was beginning to tire. Then a new opportunity literally dropped into my lap. I was asked to teach a class of teenage girls. It was a job that seemed to fit better with my personality. I have always loved to be in charge of things, and people had told me I had a knack for teaching. Besides that, I was convinced that this act of service would make a major difference in other people's lives—for Jesus' sake.

I worked hard at this new venture. I spent hours each week in preparation and came to the class on Sundays with pages of notes and visual aids tucked under my arm. But for some reason, my message received a less-than-enthusiastic response. Sunday after Sunday, my students sat huddled in a circle looking bored, while I went on and on about spiritual truths that were way over my own head.

I was about to give up when I witnessed a burst of enthu-siasm from one of my girls. The experience literally changed the course of my life. Right in the middle of the lesson, this young lady moved to the edge of her chair, sucked in a big gulp of air, and waved her arms. My heart beat wildly, as I thought we'd finally connected. A hush settled over the group, and I waited and wondered what I'd said to impress her so. My bubble of euphoria burst when she pointed a well-manicured finger at her friend on the other side of the circle, opened her mouth wide, and gushed, "If those are not the cutest shoes I've ever seen! Where did you get those shoes?" (I know, it's funny now, but at the time the emotion I felt was definitely not humor!)

After a full week of soul-searching, I decided to resign my teaching position and join a group where I could learn from an older, mature teacher, a woman named Johanna. Sitting in her classroom, I couldn't help but notice that she didn't seem overworked or stressed at all. Her unique methods of imparting truth as well as her warm, mentoring style made a deep impression on me. But more than anything else, I noticed in her an overflowing joy coupled with a love for truth and an almost mystical devotion to Jesus. At times she was literally overcome with emotion as she read from the Bible. "Oh," she'd cry, "this is wonderful!" At other times her voice would take on a deeply reverent tone. "I should take off my shoes, for this is holy ground."

Since I'd grown up in the church, I knew the importance of the Scriptures. I even knew the meaning of the words "inspired" and "inerrant." And I believed the Bible to be true—literally, from Genesis to Maps. But to be honest, I

WHO, ME?

The next time you feel old, washed up, or as if God can't use you, just remember . . .

Noah was a drunk.

Abraham was too old.

Isaac was a daydreamer.

Jacob was a liar.

Leah was ugly.

Joseph was abused.

Moses had a stuttering problem.

Gideon was afraid.

Samson was a womanizer.

Rahab was a prostitute.

Jeremiah and Timothy were too young.

David had an affair and was a murderer.

Elijah was suicidal.

Isaiah preached naked.

Jonah ran from God.

Naomi was a widow.

Job went bankrupt.

John the Baptist ate bugs.

Peter denied Christ.

The disciples fell asleep while praying.

Martha worried about everything.

Mary Magdalene was, well, you know . . .

The Samaritan woman was divorced . . . more than once!

Zacchaeus was too small.

Paul was too religious.

Timothy had an ulcer.

Lazarus was dead![2]

didn't *love* the Bible, at least not with the kind of fervor Johanna had. I wondered why. It didn't take me long to figure out that maybe I didn't know much about the Bible. How could I love a book I'd never read? Oh, I'd read bits and pieces—a passage that related to my Sunday school lesson or a verse highlighted in a devotional book, but I'd never read it through. I decided it was time to see what the Bible was all about.

Marching into the tiny bookstore in downtown Greenville, I treated myself to a brand-new, black leather version with gilded pages. When I got home, I took it out of the box and wrote my name inside. That night I began reading in Genesis. A few days later I started Exodus. Before long I found myself completely mystified by Leviticus and, later, bogged down in Numbers. But by the time I reached Deuteronomy, I was completely caught up in the drama. To borrow one of Johanna's exclamations, "It was wonderful!" There were a few times I even felt an urge to "take off my shoes."

As I continued to read, I began to understand what "inspired" really meant—that every word of Scripture, though written by some human pen, came directly from God, that it was literally "breathed out"[3] from his very essence. But now I'd come to a deeply personal, albeit simple, understanding. Because the Bible was inspired or breathed out by God, it was "alive" and able to breathe new life into me. In the five months it took me to read the Bible through, the words—God's living words[4]—literally changed my life from the inside out. I was completely caught up, not only in a pursuit of truth, but also in the One who embodies truth.[5] I grew not just in Bible knowledge but in my knowledge of him as well.

Eventually I would teach a class again, but not to change the world or pay back some spiritual debt I owed. I had been filled to the brim with the purest form of love and joy I'd ever known or thought possible, and I just wanted to tell somebody—anybody who would listen—what I'd learned. I could no more hold it back than I could stop the Jordan River from overflowing its banks.

Throughout this spiritual journey, Johanna had stayed close by, assuming the role of spiritual mentor (or spiritual mom) to me. When I was confused over a certain passage, she helped me find the information I needed in a Bible dictionary or other reference book. She often dropped by my house, leaving books, small gifts, or encouraging notes in my mailbox. Sometimes we talked on the phone, rejoicing together over some of my simple discoveries and sharing her deeper insights.

Even with Johanna's active family and other responsibilities, she still managed to find time for me. She accomplished this by taking advantage of whatever spare moments she had. I rode in the car with her as she visited her Sunday school members. We talked in the parking lot after church. Occasionally we walked along the country roads near her cabin on the lake and talked about everything from families to problem texts in Hebrews. In short, Johanna embraced me as a friend—just as I was. During those months, we bonded deeply. Because Johanna knew I looked up to her, she warned, "Don't imitate me, Gracie. Just be yourself and follow Jesus."

As I pondered what it meant to follow Jesus, I realized I was not called to meet every need that I heard about, not even those I was well equipped to do. Even Jesus did not meet every need made known to him. Instead, he carefully followed his Father's will, obeying—one step at a time—after it became crystal clear what God wanted him to do. I finally understood that Jesus had not saved me so I could serve him. He had saved me from sin, and with that barrier removed, it became possible for us to have intimate fellowship. He had saved me so we could be friends.[6]

After that moment of epiphany, whenever I heard of a need or was asked to serve in a particular area, I responded, "Give me time to consider this," or "I need to pray about that need." Later, at home, away from the pressure of a needy ministry, I tested the waters. Was this opportunity one for me to pursue, or was I called to do something else? I decided that by jumping into every sea of activity, I might be keeping another person from a ministry that suited his or her special talents and gifts. When I stepped back and learned to say no to opportunities that were uncomfortable for me, I was amazed at those who stepped forward and assumed roles and accepted responsibilities I had previously felt compelled to do.

When I learned to think and pray before diving headfirst into every project, I was able to relax and enjoy my relationship with God. An incredible reality dawned on me. I was deeply loved by the sovereign God of the universe, and his love was unconditional. That meant that he loved me, loved *me*—not what I was able to accomplish or create. For several months I rested upon the still, deep waters of solitude, spending lots of time swinging on the porch, walking in the woods, communing with Deity.

I didn't know it at the time, but this period of rest was preparation for a richer, fuller ministry than I ever could have imagined. One that would require only a small investment of my time and energy, but one that would pay huge dividends. Like ripples that go out when a tiny pebble is tossed into the water, some of the blessings continue to this day.

One day the phone rang. It was Nancy, a young woman I knew in our Bible study group. "Gracie," she said timidly, "I was just wondering if . . . maybe, I could talk to you about something."

SAGE LANGUAGE FOR ANY AGE

Do you realize that the only time in our lives when we like to get old is when we're kids?

If you're less than ten years, you're so excited about aging that you think in fractions. "How old are you?" "I'm four-and-a-half!" Why is it we never hear anyone say, "I'm thirty-six-and-a-half"?

You get into your teens, now they can't hold you back. You jump to the next number. "How old are you?" "I'm gonna be sixteen." You could be twelve, but you're gonna be sixteen.

Then the greatest day of your life happens. You become twenty-one. Even the words sound like a ceremony—*twenty-one! Yes!*

Eventually you turn thirty. Oh, what happened there? Suddenly you sound like bad milk. "He turned. We had to throw him out." There's no fun now. What's wrong? What changed?

You're pushing forty. "It's all uphill now." Then you reach fifty. Suddenly your dreams are gone. You make it to sixty . . . but you didn't think you'd make it. Before you know it, you've built up so much speed you've hit seventy.

After that, it's a day-by-day thing. You hit Wednesday. Smack. By lunch, you've run into eighty.

Funny thing, though, by ninety you start going backwards. "I was just ninety-two!" And a stranger thing happens next. You make it to one hundred and you become a little kid again: "I'm one-hundred-and-a-half!"[7]

When we met later in the week, she explained, "I was brought up in the church, but now, well . . . it seems I don't remember a thing I learned. Could you teach me how to study the Bible?"

Well, yeah!

After that conversation, Nancy and I met together regularly, and *I* assumed the role of spiritual mentor to my young friend. I found time by following the pattern that Johanna had taught me. I simply fit her into my previously planned activities. "I usually go for a walk every morning at seven. Could you join me then?"

The next morning, Nancy's car pulled into my driveway just as I was lacing up my tennis shoes. Twice a week for many weeks we walked along the country roads close to my house and talked about the Bible, our spiritual goals, and our families.

One morning Nancy revealed the unmet longing of her heart. "I want to have children, but so far the tests have been negative. What if I never have them?"

I promised to pray for her.

Imagine my joy when, a few months later, she called after a doctor's visit. "Gracie," she whooped, "I'm pregnant!" Two years later she called again—with the same message. A couple of years after that, ditto. When I heard that third announcement, I couldn't hold back a mischievous giggle as I responded, "Whenever you're ready, I'll stop praying."

The nice thing about mentoring others is that it doesn't demand a seminary degree or an ordained position in the church. (And, no, you don't have to read the Bible all the way through to be qualified. That's just something that I wanted to do!) All that's really required is that a person be open, available, and ready to pour God's love into another life. Then, in time, the mentor will receive the blessing of watching that life go on to spread love to others who spread love to others and—you get the incredible picture. It's a far-reaching, life-changing, eternal gift that any woman of any age can give.

If you have been a follower of Christ for many years, you've probably been involved in some kind of Christian ministry. Perhaps, like me, you've overdone it at times. And now that you are moving into the second half of life, you're ready to sit back, rest, and enjoy your leisure. Maybe since your children are grown you are thinking about retirement, or at least living life at a much slower pace. Some of you may be looking forward to traveling or settling in a retirement village.

While the circumstances of our lives may ebb and flow like the tide, some things never change. Such is the eternal truth that flows from the pen of the apostle Paul: "Let the word of Christ dwell in you richly as you teach and admonish one another with all wisdom, and as you sing psalms, hymns and spiritual songs with gratitude in your hearts to God."[8] Thankfully there are as many ways to follow his instruction as there are different personalities, talents, and spiritual gifts.

For me, it means spending at least some of my spare time with a younger (or newer) Christian. What better way for a woman to create a splash that will shower God's love and grace over future generations?

7

God Is Not Finished with Me Yet!

FINDING MEANING IN EVERYDAY STUFF

> I am like a little pencil in His hand. That is all. He does the thinking. He does the writing. The pencil has nothing to do with it. The pencil has only to be allowed to be used.
>
> Mother Teresa

After she and her husband retired, it didn't take Cynthia long to decide she would not spend the rest of her days sitting in a rocking chair, idling away her time. For one thing, she'd continue working in the beautiful gardens that surrounded her house. She also planned to keep tending the flowerbeds that graced the storefront of her daughter's business, Cherry's Christian Bookstore.

91

Cynthia's gardening at the bookstore was her own unique sort of ministry, blessing the hearts of Cherry's customers for more than twenty years.

One bright spring afternoon, I pulled into the parking lot and noticed Cynthia chopping weeds among the rosebushes lining the driveway. She was decked out in loose-fitting blue jeans, a long-sleeved checkered shirt, and floral gardening gloves. Her wide-brimmed straw hat, cocked slightly to one side, was perched atop her stylishly cut, salt-and-pepper hair.

When she recognized me, she leaned against her hoe and motioned for me to come over. "Want a cutting off this bush?" she asked. "It's an antique rose. Just smell the fragrance."

I stooped to sniff the heavenly aroma, cupping the perfectly formed bud in my hand.

"Today's hybrids," Cynthia said, "just don't have the fragrance that an antique rose has. This bush grew from a cutting right off a bush in my yard."

"It's wonderful," I murmured as a feeling of contentment washed over me—aromatherapy for my soul. "I'll forgo the cutting," I added and stifled a laugh. The thought that I, a woman who had killed at least one of every plant species known to man, could grow a rosebush from a cutting was downright funny. For the next few minutes, I admired the other rosebushes and listened to Cynthia talk about the different kinds of flowers in the bed.

Then the conversation changed directions. "Did I tell you I'm helping out in the store now?" Cynthia cut a long-stemmed pink rose and started removing the thorns. "Every Friday morning I vacuum the carpet and dust the glass shelves that hold the figurines. Just being around Cherry's customers brightens my day, especially when they compliment the flowerbeds. And my daughter is glad she doesn't have to clean all those display cases." Cynthia removed her gloves and handed me the rose.

"Here, put this in a bud vase when you get home. It should last several days. Just cut the stem at an angle and add a little fresh water every morning."

I thanked her and then cradled the bloom in my hand, protecting it from the brisk April breeze, as I headed toward the store.

Once inside, I mentioned my conversation with Cynthia to Cherry. "I hear your mother is putting her special touch on things inside of the store as well as in the garden." I smiled when I thought about Cherry's mother, an energetic seventy-year-old woman with no time for just piddling around.

"Yes, she's been a great help," Cherry said, "but you should ask her what happened last week. She has an interesting story to tell."

I couldn't wait to find out exactly what had happened. That evening I poured myself a cup of coffee, settled in my recliner, and called Cynthia. Never one for beating around the rosebush, I jump-started the conversation. "Cherry says you have a story to tell me. I'm all ears."

"Well," she began, "I usually come to work early in the morning, about 7:00, and of course, I keep the doors locked while I clean. But on this particular morning, I must have had a 'senior moment.' It didn't take me long to discover my mistake. I was going about my regular routine, vacuuming in the back of the store, when I glanced up and spotted a man standing by the cash register. My heart stopped!"

"Oh, Cynthia! What did you do?" As she gathered her thoughts, I tried to imagine the uneasy scene. "You must have been scared to death!"

"Actually, for some reason, I didn't feel scared," Cynthia said. "In all my years working at the bookstore, I never met a person I didn't like. I guess that's why I didn't panic at the sight of the intruder. I just stood my ground and gave him the once over."

I took a big gulp of the warm coffee from the mug I cupped in my hand as Cynthia filled in the details.

The man was dressed in faded blue jeans and a tattered, sleeveless shirt with missing buttons. Cynthia could see that his chest and arms were literally covered with dark blue, crimson, and green tattoos. His dark hair was pulled back in a curly ponytail and fastened with a rubber band. When the man turned his head, she noticed he had a gold earring. "At first he seemed startled too," Cynthia said, "but then he cleared his throat and spoke."

make a Splash

HELPING HANDS

I recently heard of a woman who spent her midlife years working for an organization that delivers lunches to elderly shut-ins. Occasionally the woman takes her four-year-old granddaughter with her on the noontime rounds. The child was unfailingly intrigued by the various appliances used by some of the oldsters—particularly the canes, walkers, and wheelchairs.

One day the lady noticed her granddaughter staring at a pair of false teeth soaking in a glass. As she braced herself for the inevitable barrage of questions, the child merely turned and whispered, "The tooth fairy will never believe this!"

"This your purse sitting here on the counter, ma'am?"

Cynthia glanced at the purse and nodded her head yes. Her heart pounded as she thought, *How could I have been so careless?* Cynthia's usual routine always included tucking her purse underneath the counter in an out-of-the-way place. But on this particular day, as an April shower pelted the sidewalk outside, she'd pushed through the door, plopped her purse on the counter, and ran straight to the bathroom to towel off her blouse.

"I must have forgotten to put my purse away," Cynthia said, "and obviously, I forgot to flip the deadbolt on the front door. When I came out of the bathroom, I headed for the closet that held the vacuum cleaner without giving my purse a second thought."

Though the episode had taken place several days before, Cynthia was breathing rapidly as she picked up the story once more. "I was startled by the man's question, so I gave the purse a closer look. It was gaping open with my wallet sticking out of the top. The man could have easily grabbed it and run off with my grocery money—to say nothing of my credit cards and all my personal identification. I wondered why he hadn't. Instead, he matter-of-factly suggested, 'You ought to put that away.' Then his voice softened as he added, 'Don't be scared, ma'am. I won't hurt you. I walked over from the bus station 'cause the sign said Christian Bookstore. Somethin' sort of drew me to come. Because, well . . . I'm a Christian.'"

Cynthia took a deep breath and walked toward the man. *Is this guy for real?* she wondered. His arms were folded tightly in what seemed to be a self-conscious effort to cover the tear in his shirt or maybe to hide the smear of grease on the front. In spite of his frightful appearance, a sense of peace prevailed in Cynthia's heart. "He didn't look like a criminal," she said, "but rather out of place, like a lost child trying to find his way home."

"Then what happened?" I asked, swirling the coffee in my mug as if trying to hasten the story toward its finale.

"I told him, 'I believe you.' Then I stepped closer and said, 'I don't think you'll hurt me. Can I do something to help you?' The young man shifted uncomfortably, then told me what he wanted."

"I just got out of a drug rehab center last week," the man said, "and I'm on my way home." He explained his newfound relationship with God. "After detox, I found out about Jesus. I need to stay close to him so I can stay off drugs. Maybe you could give me a book or something?"

"My mind raced," Cynthia said. She knew that Cherry often gave away books and tracts to people who needed them. Sometimes she even gave a leather study Bible to new converts. She wondered what Cherry would give him if she were in the store right now? Several ideas played about in her mind. Her eyes scanned the titles on a nearby bookshelf. "Now I was the one feeling lost and uncomfortable," she said. "I didn't have a clue where to find books for recovering addicts." Cynthia breathed a quick prayer, and suddenly, like a voice from heaven, an idea came clearly.

Earlier that morning when she pulled out of her driveway, she remembered stopping at her mailbox before heading down the country road toward town. When she removed the loose bundle of mail from the box, she had noticed her favorite Christian magazine, one known for its stories about people whose lives had changed dramatically—even when they were once out of control or full of pain. These stories always encouraged Cynthia to trust God even in the most adverse circumstances. She pushed her purse under the counter and told the man, "This is not my store. I just clean on Fridays.

But if you'll come outside with me, I'll give you something that came in this morning's mail."

When Cynthia opened the door and motioned for the man to follow her, she was struck by the beautiful morning sunshine peeking over the tops of the trees. Puddles on the parking lot sparkled like diamonds in the radiant light. The brilliance of sunshine after rain! To Cynthia, it seemed a reflection of God's favor and grace.

Standing beside her car, both the young intruder and the courageous oldster seemed to feel more at ease. Cynthia talked to the young man freely about his new life in Christ. "There may be times when you doubt whether or not God is with you. Maybe you will even question his existence. But he will never leave you. No matter where you are or what is happening, God is there. He is all around you, just as the sunshine is all around us right now. Don't ever be afraid to call on him." Cynthia encouraged him to go to church when he got home. "It will help you to be around other people who believe in God." Then she shuffled through the stack of mail and handed him the magazine. "I think God wants me to give you this. Maybe one of these stories will help."

He leafed through the pages, then broke into a big grin.

"He must have spotted something he needed," Cynthia said, "but I had no idea what it was."

He folded the magazine and shoved it into his pocket. "I'll read it on the bus," he said. "You've helped me more than you'll ever know."

At this point there was a long pause as I held the receiver and waited for Cynthia to continue. When she finally spoke, I could tell she was choking back tears. "Oh, Gracie, then the most amazing thing happened."

"Go on," I urged. "I'm sitting on the edge of my recliner."

"Well," she said, "our eyes connected for just a moment. Then he stooped and kissed me on the cheek. After that, he turned and walked away. I couldn't help but notice a bounce in his step as he crossed the street. Just before he reached the bus station, he looked over his shoulder and shouted, 'Hallelujah! God bless you!'

"Gracie, my heart beat with joy as I waved good-bye to him. Somehow I knew that on that ordinary day, God had trusted me with a divine encounter. A recovering drug addict had faced the temptation to steal and had passed the test. And a busy old lady had faced a frightful-looking intruder with God's grace and peace."

Later that evening on her way home from work, Cynthia stopped by to visit with her sister. "I wanted to tell her about my experience," she explained. "Gracie, there on the coffee table was a copy of the magazine I had given to that young man. I couldn't wait to open it up and try to figure out which story had captured his interest. I leafed through the pages and spotted one about a recovering drug addict who designed stained glass windows.

"In the article, a man named Timothy described his changed life. 'With God as my focal point, other aspects of my life fell into place day by day. Hard times that formerly would have sent me to drugs now send me to the Bible. I began reading Scripture and praying. I was not only shaking my habit, I was also shaking my old attitudes and behaviors along with it. In the same way that pieces of stained glass come alive when lifted to the light, I was allowing God's light to illuminate my own darkness.'"[1]

"Oh, Cynthia, what a perfect story to follow up what you said to him earlier." I thought about God's awesome ways of working. Even though we make our plans day by day, it is really he who is in charge of the events that take place.[2]

It was certainly no accident that Timothy's story was in the magazine that came in the mail that day. Even the fact that Cynthia decided to pick up her mail on her way into town instead of waiting until after work seemed prearranged by God's hand.

I brushed away a tear. The idea that the eternal God concerns himself with my schedule as I live out my life here in the confines of time, and that he does this with great interest and care, boggled my mind, warmed my heart, and brought joy to my soul.

"In the days since my experience with that young man," Cynthia said, "I have wondered if our brief encounter touched his life as deeply as it did mine. In my heart I know that God had used me—me, an old lady who tends flowerbeds—to fertilize and water new life in a person who needed to grow. I may never know what happens to that man, but I will keep on praying for him. I'll ask God to help him, just as he helped Timothy to shake his old habits, to stay off drugs, and to keep his mind focused on spiritual things."

Cynthia paused, then added thoughtfully, "And when I pray for myself, I ask God to help me not be afraid of people or too tired to help. When I get too busy to notice the needs of other people, I want him to interrupt me, just like he did that day in the store. You know, Gracie, I want to stay involved and make a difference in the lives of others—for all the days of my life."

Recently my pastor, Andy McQuitty, said something that made an impression on me. It's a statement that should provide perfect peace for all of us whenever we find ourselves in some sort of precarious or frightening situation.

The following test found in Barbara Johnson's book *Leaking Laffs Between Pampers and Depends* reminds us of some things that have disappeared from the scene with the turn of the century—or before. See which ones you remember:

Blackjack chewing gum
Little Coke-shaped bottles made of wax with colored sugar water inside
Soda pop machines that dispensed glass bottles
Home milk delivery in glass bottles with cardboard caps
Telephone party lines
Newsreels before movies
P.F. Flyers
Butch wax
Telephone numbers with a word prefix (Olive 2-6933 or Tuxedo 4-9351)
Peashooters
Howdy Doody
45 RPM and 78 RPM records
Metal ice trays with levers
Mimeograph machines
Blue flashbulbs
Beanie and Cecil
Roller-skate keys
Cork popguns
Studebakers
Wringer washtubs
Count how many of these items you remember to know how old you really are:
0—You're still young
1-10—You're getting older
11-15—Don't tell your age
More than 15—You're older than dirt![3]

"I know that my days are predetermined by God,"[4] he remarked after he had stepped to the front of the platform. He grinned. "Until God is finished with me, I am indestructible. When it's time for me to go, it's indisputable." Then he pushed his hands deep into his pockets, shrugged his shoulders, and said, "That's why I ride motorcycles."

I laughed along with the rest of the audience attending Irving Bible Church that Sunday morning. But even though the words were humorous, they have stayed with me to this day. May they abide in your heart as well!

Be courageous, adventurous women. You are totally safe in the hands of our all-powerful, sovereign God, and he's not finished with you yet.

8

Navigating Troubled Waters

DEALING WITH DECLINING HEALTH

I wonder if we honestly realize the rich resources which God
provides when He takes away our health or certain coveted
abilities. We may think we could do far more with more,
but God knows He can do a great deal more in our lives
with a good deal less.

Joni Eareckson Tada

When we lived in Paris, Texas, one of the first
couples my husband, Joe, and I met were Larry
and Marilyn Miears. We became fast friends even
though to an outsider it must have seemed an unlikely
union. For one thing, Larry was band director at Paris High
School, and Joe, being technically minded, had very little
musical talent. Besides that, Joe and I were several years
older than the young couple.

Nevertheless, we bonded closely, mostly because Larry doted on our twelve-year-old son, Mike, and Marilyn was infatuated with our baby boy, Jason. Since Marilyn was pregnant, most of our early conversations revolved around taking care of our babies. But before long, the relationship between the four of us grew and deepened. It included weighty discussions about theological issues and late-night jam sessions during which Larry pounded out show tunes on the piano or played jazz on his trumpet. Usually an evening with Larry and Marilyn concluded with old-fashioned camp meeting songs or well-known hymns that we sang in four-part harmony as we gathered around the piano in their living room.

We were together during some of life's crucial moments as well. I'll never forget the night Marilyn went into labor. All four of us were singing in the choir during a special presentation at our church. Marilyn was standing among a group of sopranos, and I was at the other end of the loft with the altos. Somewhere in the back row, Joe and Larry stood side by side in a long line of tenors.

Suddenly, right between the second and third stanzas of "Higher Ground," I heard a rather loud "psst" coming from the soprano section. I leaned forward so I could see around a row of tummies and spotted Marilyn. She mouthed the words, "It's time!"

I mouthed back, "Now?"

"Now!" she persisted. Then with a swoop of her hand, she motioned for me to join her in the wings.

She slipped out the left door, and I pushed my way through the door on the right. After a few pertinent questions behind the scenes, I decided she was absolutely right. It was time! We needed to fetch Larry and Joe.

I opened the door and caught the attention of the guy on the end of the tenor row. Marilyn and I couldn't hold back the giggles—between the pains, of course—as one guy nudged another, and another, then another, until Larry finally got the message. He let out a whoop and grabbed Joe by the arm. They climbed over the other men and made their way to the door. We were so excited as we removed our robes and gathered our belongings that another tenor left the choir and came out to shush us. For some reason, we even found that funny. We laughed excitedly as we went outside, got into our respective cars, and drove as fast as we could to St. Joseph Hospital.

I guess we'll never know how much we disrupted the services that evening, but Marilyn and I talked about it later. We decided that most people hadn't heard a thing the preacher said. We knew for sure we had disturbed most of our cronies, for dozens of them gathered in the parking lot at the hospital where they kept a vigil most of the night. Joe and I stayed right outside the labor room on the second floor so we could encourage Marilyn and wipe Larry's brow as the contractions increased and the pain sharpened. Every few minutes one of us would go out on the porch and shout a status report to the waiting crowd. Finally, when little Brian was born, a party broke out. Horns honked and everyone shared bubblegum cigars.

After a couple of years, Larry took a position in another town, and even though we vowed to keep in touch, we only did so at Christmas or on certain occasions when they drove through Paris on the way to Oklahoma to visit their family. During these years, Larry and Marilyn added two more children to their family. To be honest, I was not quite sure how they managed to do that without my help. Nevertheless,

GOD-SIZED GIFTS

No matter how troubled the waters we are navigating, God always shows up with unexpected gifts of love:

There once was a little boy who wanted to meet God. He knew it was a long trip to where God lived, so he packed his suitcase with Twinkies and a six-pack of root beer. Then he started his journey. When he had gone about three blocks, he met an old man. He was sitting in the park, just staring at some pigeons.

The boy sat down next to him and opened his suitcase. He was about to take a drink from his root beer when he noticed that the old man looked hungry, so he offered him a Twinkie. The man gratefully accepted it and smiled at him. His smile was so incredible that the boy wanted to see it again, so he offered him a root beer. Once again, the old man smiled. The boy was delighted! They sat there for a long while eating and smiling, but they never said a word. Finally the little boy realized how tired he was, and he got up to leave. But before he had gone more than a few steps, he turned around, ran back to the old man, and gave him a hug. The old man gave him his biggest smile ever.

When the boy opened the door to his own house a short time later, his mother was surprised by the look of joy on his face. She asked him, "What did you do today that made you so happy?" He replied, "I had lunch with God." But before his mother could respond, he added, "You know what? He's got the most beautiful smile I've ever seen!"

Meanwhile, the old man, also radiant with joy, returned to his home. His son was stunned by the look of peace on his face, and he asked, "Father, what did you do today that made you so happy?" He replied, "I ate Twinkies in the park with God." But before his son responded, he added, "You know, he's much younger than I expected."[1]

their Jason and little Rachel were indisputable proof that these two were getting along just fine without Mama Gracie and Papa Joe.

Eventually we moved too, from Paris back to Greenville—the place where our roots grew deep into East Texas soil. Imagine our surprise and delight when a few years later we heard that Larry was being interviewed for the high school band director position in Greenville.

They'd no sooner moved to town and unpacked their boxes than they showed up at our front door bearing a bottle of Pepsi and a bag of Doritos. Such was the nature of our friendship. It was a come-as-you-are, bring-what-you've-got, stay-as-long-as-you-like kind of deal. They walked in, and we took up right where we'd left off a few years before. We laughed, we played, we sang, as if only a few days had lapsed between visits.

Larry and Marilyn had been living in Greenville for several months when our family began wading through some rather murky waters. Now don't even try to figure what went wrong. Just imagine your worst day and realize that we felt exactly that low. Even Larry and Marilyn didn't try to figure out the details. They just showed up. I opened the front door to a knock one evening, and there they stood with a bottle of Pepsi tucked under Larry's arm. That evening there was no singing as we sat huddled around our table, talking quietly, praying together.

A couple of years passed before we heard that Marilyn was ill. We knew it was serious. So we did the only thing we knew to do. We bought a bottle of Pepsi and drove over to their house. We pulled our chairs close to the table as Marilyn began to fill us in on the details. The following account, as told to me by Marilyn, describes two incredible years when this family learned to navigate the troubled waters of adversity.

We celebrated my birthday on a beautiful Saturday with friends. What more could a person want? Larry's job left us very little time for leisure activities, but we decided that since the children were growing up—Brian was in college and Jason and Rachel in high school—it was time to create a few waves in the rather placid waters of our lives. An afternoon of tennis doubles seemed a good beginning.

Larry suggested I play on his left because of his weak backhand. As we played, I managed to cover for him, returning almost every ball that came to my right. But the balls that came to my left seemed to disappear in the air, like someone was plucking them from the sky then dropping them to the ground. I shook my head and wondered, *What's wrong with my eyes?*

The next morning I made an appointment with my optometrist. After a quick exam, he said I had an "internal problem" and should see an ophthalmologist. The following day the vision field exam made me sick, and the ophthalmologist suggested I go immediately to my regular doctor. I felt confident that Sheila, my close friend and family physician, could fix whatever was wrong. Then I heard him call ahead, suggesting a CAT scan.

By the time I got to Sheila's office, I realized this wasn't something easily "fixed." I couldn't hold back an outburst of emotion as I asked, "What's happening to me?"

Sheila tried to appear confident, but I noticed tears in her eyes when she hugged me. "Let's see what the test reveals."

A few days later as I waited at home for the results, I heard a car in the driveway. I looked out the window and saw Sheila jump from her car and bound down the sidewalk. When she opened the front door, she grabbed me in a big bear hug and announced, "There is a tumor, but the location indicates it's benign. I think we can treat it with medication or surgery. Of course, we'll need further tests."

Talk about mixed emotions! I felt a weird combination of relief—it probably was not cancer, but I was also scared and confused, like I was wandering through a maze not knowing which way to turn. Cresting the waves of conflicting emotion was a deep-seated awareness of God's presence. It seemed as if he was taking me by the hand to lead me through deep waters.

Sheila consulted with another doctor, then set up an appointment with another ophthalmologist. Since Larry had to attend a band concert that day, Patti, a close friend, accompanied me. Painful eye and vision exams lasted all day. At 7:00 p.m. we were still waiting for a report when an intern came in with a somber expression, placed his hand on my shoulder, and said, "Good-bye and good luck."

Something about his tone of voice caused me to know I was in big trouble. I burst into tears. "Patti, I want to go home, leave this all here, and never see it again!" I wanted to run away from the doctors, the fears, the tears, and even from my hurting family. With each new doctor, the prognosis had worsened. Patti comforted me before the doctor entered the room. "Mrs. Miears," he began soberly, "we've carefully examined your CAT scan and found the reason for your recent visual problems." My heart pounded as the doctor continued calmly, "A tumor is destroying your field of vision in both eyes."

The next day, Larry went with me for a brain scan in Dallas. The results confirmed my greatest fear. "See these jagged edges?" the doctor asked, pointing to the films on his office view box. "This is malignant."

My heart sank, my eyes dropped, and I felt numb. I wanted to scramble for Larry's lap, like I did with Daddy when I got hurt as a little girl.

When I looked up, the doctor's clear blue eyes communicated strength and confidence. "We will fight, and we will win, won't we?"

I wasn't sure. I knew fighting meant lots of money. Unfortunately, in another bizarre turn of events, we had recently changed insurance companies. The new policy was not in effect yet.

Larry broke the news. "We don't have insurance."

The doctor paused a moment, then said, "We can't wait on this. We'll work out the finances later. As for me," he added, "I can donate my services. I'll check with the anesthesiologist and the hospital."

I couldn't believe what the doctor had just indicated. Knowing the cost would be reduced was wonderful news, but my emotions did another flip-flop when he explained the procedure and possible complications, including blindness, disability, or paralysis. "The surgery will need to be done right away," he explained.

Driving from Dallas to our home in Greenville, we didn't talk much. We stopped at Lake Ray Hubbard and walked hand in hand along the shoreline. At times we cried in each other's arms. "What is happening?" "What are we going to do?" "What about the kids?" As we talked, one thing became clear: we would live our lives only moment by moment.

After arriving home, Larry called a few of our closest friends, who came immediately. They sat around the table, encouraging, praying, crying, sometimes not saying a word.

When our three teenagers got home, we included them in the circle and explained the situation.

That night I cried out to God, "Please, stop this! I can't do this." I just wanted a normal life, to feel good, to cook, to hug my kids, and to be their mom. The devastating news seemed to open up a lot of old wounds. Life is not fair! Feelings of frustration and bitterness played about in my mind as I thought back to my childhood.

When I was eleven, my daddy received a head injury playing football with my brothers. He spent his last ten years in a coma. While Mama cared for him, I took on most of the household chores. Every day before school, I washed clothes, hung them outside, and cooked breakfast. Afterward I did homework and cooked supper. Mama worked hard, growing vegetables in our hothouse to provide a meager income.

Not knowing how to handle such incredible difficulties and stress, I let my emotions control me. I felt angry that other girls had nice things and carefree lives. I resented some of the women in our neighborhood who criticized Mama for working on Sunday. I feared the "welfare lady" who called on us regularly, threatening to take possession of our house. The way I handled my feelings became a destructive pattern that continued to plague me as an adult.[2]

In spite of these negative thoughts, before bedtime, as I pondered my past and prayed about my future, I felt an unexplainable peace. My spirit remained peaceful throughout the following days. When friends hugged me and cried, I could honestly say, "I'll be okay; God is good." I knew, whatever the outcome, God was in control.

The next day the hospital informed us they would charge a flat fee of ten thousand dollars. Larry and I decided we could borrow that much. Surgery was scheduled, and I tried to get organized just in case God decided to take me home. I gave my children a crash course on how to wash their clothes and cook. One day I told Larry that I thought he should remarry. I even made a list of possible candidates, which he promptly discarded, saying, "But you're going to be around fifty or sixty years!" Throughout this time of preparation, I often wondered why I felt so calm. I should have been weeping and fearful. The only answer was God's peace and joy.

My friends visited me often, providing encouragement, words of comfort, prayers, and practical help, including money. One day one of our friends came by, handed Larry an envelope, and said, "Some folks wanted to help with expenses." Inside was a check for ten thousand dollars! We couldn't believe our eyes. One Sunday at church, an usher pressed some money into Larry's palm as they shook hands. Larry glanced down and saw a twenty-dollar bill. Later he realized it was five twenty-dollar bills folded together! Overwhelmed by the generosity of our Christian friends, I checked into the hospital feeling encouraged and blessed.

Surgery went smoothly. When the doctor emerged to give Larry a report, an anxious hush settled over the crowd of family and friends that filled two large waiting rooms. Later the doctor said, "I felt like E. F. Hutton. When I talked, everybody listened." He had removed most of the tumor. The biopsy results would take several weeks.

I awoke in a beautiful hospital suite surrounded by fresh flowers and smiling faces. I ran my fingers through my long thick hair the doctors had painstakingly preserved. Larry was with me looking rested and confident. I learned later that another friend had given him three hundred dollars, saying, "Stay nearby in a nice motel." Throughout my recovery from surgery, visitors encouraged me.

When I got home, our friends had redecorated our bedroom. New curtains, a quilted bedspread, and new fluffy pillows made me feel like a queen. They had even planted a rose garden in my backyard. I couldn't believe my eyes. Why did my friends love me so much? I certainly didn't deserve it! Their love was unconditional and abundant.

That evening as I prayed, God spoke to my heart: "Your friends are expressing my love. They love you because I love you." Tears of joy flowed freely as I basked in the warm glow of God's presence. Since that day, I've never doubted God's love. I was able to let go of my accumulated bitterness. It was like releasing balloons into the wind. I felt new freedom as God's amazing love replaced my fear and frustration.[3]

The biopsy showed varied characteristics, making it difficult to decide on the right treatment. After much discussion with the doctors, we opted for radiation. Again our friends insisted on "the best"—outpatient treatment at M. D. Anderson Hospital in Houston.

When Larry and I arrived, someone had rented an apartment for us in a secure complex with shuttle service (and four swimming pools). It was beautifully decorated and equipped with TV, VCR, and telephones. God continued to meet my needs. When I lost a contact lens, I received a get well card the next day with fifty dollars tucked inside. And, as a special heavenly touch, a beautiful bouquet of flowers was delivered every Monday morning.

Daily in the hospital, I encountered people hurting and crippled by cancers, tumors, and other illnesses. How could I feel down or upset as I walked the halls upright and strong with no medical equipment attached? I felt so thankful, but at times I questioned God's ways.

Why does he heal some but not others? Why will some be financially ruined while our expenses are covered? Why will others struggle with loneliness on top of their pain? Since I couldn't understand, I decided to simply trust God. Maybe I needed a lavish display of his love to cover all my bitterness. I could never repay my friends, so I asked God to let me help others. And he did—several times. One situation will be etched in my memory forever.

Almost every day as I entered the waiting room, I noticed a small bald-headed boy coloring at a table or sleeping on someone's lap. Then one day in the restroom, his mother was leaning over the sink weeping uncontrollably. Feeling her sorrow and pain, I put my arms around her, trying to comfort. "Could you tell me what has upset you?"

"My son has a brain tumor," she answered.

"I have a brain tumor," I said. Her head popped up, and she hugged me and touched my hair. She seemed so excited that I was alive and healthy. For a few minutes we talked about faith, love, and courage. She appeared to have

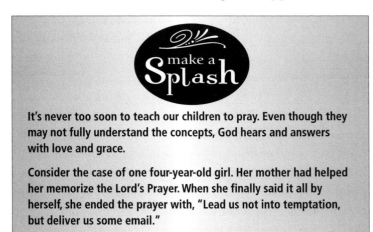

make a
Splash

It's never too soon to teach our children to pray. Even though they may not fully understand the concepts, God hears and answers with love and grace.

Consider the case of one four-year-old girl. Her mother had helped her memorize the Lord's Prayer. When she finally said it all by herself, she ended the prayer with, "Lead us not into temptation, but deliver us some email."

a new measure of hope. When she left the restroom, she walked with her shoulders straight, her head high, and a smile on her face.

After six weeks of radiation, an MRI revealed a slight growth in my tumor. But by summer I noticed an improvement in my vision and another MRI revealed a reduction. Since then I have become active in women's ministries at our church, codirecting Helping Hands, a ministry that meets the practical needs of others when they have a crisis.

Two years have passed, and another MRI is scheduled soon. We are still living our lives moment by moment, enjoying every blessing. How wonderful it is to be able to see a rainbow, enjoy my friends, walk in the falling snow, or mop a floor (and I can even use the tumor as an excuse when I forget something). Dealing with uncertainty is hard, but I am sure of one thing. Even if the tumor starts to grow again, my bitterness is gone forever. As crazy as it may sound, the tumor actually "healed" me. God touched a place deep in my soul where I needed healing most.

If you are living in the second half of life, I'm sure you've waded through some deep waters of your own. I know this for certain because we're all living in a far-from-perfect world. Besides that, if you are a follower of Christ, suffering is guaranteed.[4] It's one of those promises we don't want to claim. Yet in spite of our resistance to hard times, we've lived long enough to know such experiences help us grow spiritually and develop character and strength.

As hard as it is to understand why bad things happen to good people, we can always know what to do when they occur. Maybe, like Marilyn, you've mastered a few coping skills—like living one moment at a time. Isn't that the way we're all supposed to live? Perhaps while navigating troubled seas you've learned how precious your family is, how blessed you really are. Or it could be that you've simply learned how to comfort others with deeds of kindness, like talking to a mother in distress or delivering a bottle of pop to a hurting friend.

Today, more than eleven years after the tumor was discovered, Larry and Marilyn still live in Greenville. Larry decided to go back to school and is finishing up his doctoral degree. Brian, their oldest son, and his wife, Amy, have two children—Anna and Alyssa—who delight and bless their grandparents. Jason is working at Chase Manhattan, and Rachel is recently married. Marilyn's health is good and the tumor has not grown. She continues to lead Helping Hands.

PART 3

Pardon Me, I'm Having
a Senior Moment

9

I'm Out of My Mind—Be Back in Five Minutes

❧

DEALING WITH . . . NOW WHAT WAS IT?

I am only one, but still I am one.
I cannot do everything, but still I can do something;
and because I cannot do everything
I will not refuse to do the something that I can do.

Edward Everett Hale

Last year we sold our house in the small East Texas town of Greenville, where we'd lived for twenty-some years, and moved to the booming Dallas–Fort Worth area, settling in the city of Grapevine. It was a carefully thought-out decision. We would be living near our children and grandchildren. Joe would be taking a new job, working with our oldest son. In short, we were exchanging the security and warmth of long-term friendships in laid-back suburbia for a more complex life in the bustling Dallas–Fort Worth area.

As we settled into the strange surroundings, I often found myself thinking, *Gracie, you are out of your mind! People your age move into small towns, simplify their lives. You and Joe, on the other hand, have chosen to complicate yours. What were you thinking?*

Even with its uncertainty, there's something appealing about having a fresh start in the second half of life—different stores to explore, new friends, new church. With all that in mind, I determined that, along with my new beginnings, I was going to handle my life a bit differently. I would not, for example, put my foot in my mouth anymore. I would listen more, talk less, and I positively would not make the same kind of social blunders I'd made in small-town Greenville. I'd moved to the city, and I was going to act citified.

We'd scarcely unpacked our last box when we began trying out our new life. We went shopping in a nearby mall. The next day we met our new neighbors. And soon we began attending new churches. I wish I could say that in all these explorations I kept my vow of dignity. But alas, "We all stumble in many ways." Within a few short weeks, I'd broken most of the resolutions I'd made.

One of the first couples we met in our neighborhood was a retired preacher, Melburn, and his wife, Martha. They invited us to go to church with them. The very next Sunday morning, they came by to pick us up and sat with us in the worship service. We were grateful for their warm friendship, so I decided the next day to pay them a visit. I would autograph a copy of my latest book and hand deliver it to their door. (Handing out an unsolicited autographed copy of one's own book is not the world's humblest gesture, so perhaps the Lord decided to give me a character-building experience.)

I awakened early, showered, dried my hair, and used the curling iron, putting about a dozen tight little curls up top. Then I sprayed my hair and headed to the kitchen to refill my coffee cup. My usual routine is to let the hairspray dry while I'm doing other things, then circle back through the bathroom and pick it out. (It takes a lot of work to achieve the look I'm accustomed to!) On this particular morning, somewhere between the coffeepot and the hair pick, I must have had a "senior moment," for I bypassed the picking, grabbed my purse, located my keys, and headed out the door, book tucked under my arm.

When I arrived at the neighbor's front door, Melburn answered. I noticed he never made eye contact with me. His eyes stayed focused somewhere above my forehead. I should have given this oddity a little more thought, but instead I jumped in my car and went shopping. I was in a great mood, charged with the assurance that my long to-do list was diminishing. In the grocery store, I talked to strangers about the displays of food, cooed at babies buckled in shopping carts, and carried on a detailed conversation with the woman at the checkout stand.

Back home, I rushed inside, plopped my groceries on the kitchen counter, and ran to the bathroom. Glancing in the mirror, I saw my hair, still in slick rows of little tight curls. *Oh well,* I thought, *nobody knows me anyway.* But I have to admit, I felt a flush of embarrassment when I thought about my neighbors who did know me.

Soon after my curling disaster, I geared up our search for a church. (I could tell I was going to need prayer support and fast.) In one of those it's-a-small-world experiences, we'd

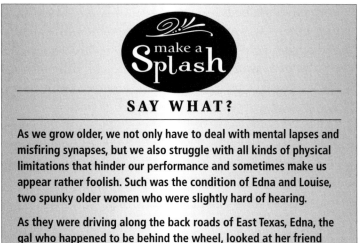

SAY WHAT?

As we grow older, we not only have to deal with mental lapses and misfiring synapses, but we also struggle with all kinds of physical limitations that hinder our performance and sometimes make us appear rather foolish. Such was the condition of Edna and Louise, two spunky older women who were slightly hard of hearing.

As they were driving along the back roads of East Texas, Edna, the gal who happened to be behind the wheel, looked at her friend sitting beside her and yelled, "Are we anywhere near Winnsboro?"

Louise shook her head and answered, "Wednesday? Heck no, it's already Thursday!"

"Thirsty? Me too," Edna bellowed as she whipped her car into the parking lot of a nearby convenience store. "Let's stop for a Coke."

learned that Terri and Rick, the daughter and son-in-law of our longtime friends Ray and Vern, lived in the area and attended church nearby. So at Vern's suggestion we all gathered one Sunday morning for worship. I knew beforehand how much Terri and Rick loved their church, and I also knew our worship experience would be what we older folk consider "nontraditional."

As expected, the preaching was inspirational, but the music, well, it was loud. Throughout the service, I noticed Terri glancing in my direction, obviously concerned that I not be overwhelmed by the volume or style of the praise choruses. Afterward in the parking lot, she draped her arm around my shoulders and asked, "Gracie, was the music too much for you?"

"Oh no," I gushed, "we really enjoyed it. . . ." If only I'd stopped there! But no, instead I blurted, "Believe me, we've heard worse!" The shocked look that crossed Terri's face stopped me dead in my conservative tracks. I cupped my hand over my mouth, and Terri burst out laughing. After the first few awkward moments, it was funny to me too.

Before long we found our place in the church we'd attended with Melburn and Martha. It was a large church with traditional worship services, one with enough room for me to keep my foot-in-mouth disease a secret. And, gratefully, my problems remained dormant for a while. That is, until Joe and I attended our first banquet.

It was a dressy affair with white tablecloths, place cards, and fresh flowers. As we entered the beautifully decorated fellowship center, I breathed a prayer: "Lord, since we're new members and all, help me not to spill something on my dress, and if at all possible, could you puhleeeze help me make a good impression on the people at my table?"

We ended up sitting beside a nice young couple, and in my usual gregarious manner, I jump-started the conversation by asking a few questions. I found out the man worked at the phone company on a new schedule—eight days of work followed by six days off. As I took a bite of my salad, I wondered what a guy would do with all that time off. Why, if a fellow were of the energetic sort, he could take up a new sport or even have another job. Then I thought about my own easygoing hubby and realized he could also sit around in a recliner or lie on the couch and do absolutely nothing. I took a sip of iced tea and, unfortunately, continued to talk. "Well," I said, "what do you do with all that free time? Do you play golf, or do you just sleep around?"

Poor Joe almost choked on his salad, and several others at the table spewed food. I quickly tried to explain what I'd just said. "Oh, I don't mean 'sleep around,'" I stammered. "I mean lie around and sleep." My voice trailed off, and I added meekly, "Of course, neither of those things is any of my business. Don't answer that question." I fidgeted with my napkin while everybody gained their composure.

The guy answered my question by saying, "Not anything that I want to talk about!" With that, the table erupted in another round of undignified guffaws and giggles. It all sounded very small-townish. And, I have to admit, for the first time since we'd moved to this giant metropolis, I felt quite at home.

A few weeks later I was in Greenville speaking to a group of ladies at our former church. Since most of the women knew me anyway, it was easy to fess up. "Gals," I began, "I may live in a new place, but I've been up to my old tricks." As I told them about the bloopers and mistakes I'd recently made, I could feel the group relax. Then it was time for me to speak on my assigned topic.

I opened my Bible and read a couple of familiar verses from a not-so-familiar translation. "Don't worry over anything whatever; tell God every detail of your needs in earnest and thankful prayer, and the peace of God, which transcends human understanding, will keep constant guard over your hearts and minds as they rest in Christ Jesus."[1]

"When we make mistakes, we're not to worry about them," I began confidently. "God is not impressed with our perfectionism. He is pleased, however, when we become real with him and with each other, and that includes admitting our failures. We're to be honest with God, telling him every detail of our needs, then we are to 'rest in Christ Jesus.' After all, we don't have to be perfect to please God. When you stumble and fall, simply get back up and start over again." I decided to illustrate the thought with a story about our five-year-old grandson, Montana.

I leaned forward on the podium, making eye contact with the audience, and in a serious tone said, "One afternoon Montana was playing in the driveway while his daddy worked on his Jet Ski. . . ." (So far so good.) In the next sentence, I tried to say that our son Mike was "tinkering on the motor." But instead, I told over a hundred women that he was "tinkling on the motor."

At this point I completely lost control of the group and, I must admit, of my own emotions, for I couldn't hold back the giggles. My touching story was put on hold, and I became a perfect example of how to handle blatant imperfection. Eventually the laughter subsided, and I straightened my face and continued. "Montana climbed on the Jet Ski and decided to step from the big vinyl seat to the storage box mounted on the rear of the trailer. Mike glanced up just as Montana stretched one little leg forward, then stumbled and fell into the space between the ski and the trailer's frame. He hit hard on the cement.

"Montana let out a scream, then burst into tears. Mike scooped him into his arms to assess the damage. He had two skinned knees, a jagged cut in his mouth, and a chipped tooth.

"It's amazing how resilient little boys can be," I said. "Before long, Montana was bandaged up and playing again. After a few minutes, Mike saw him climb back on the trailer and position himself on the seat of the Jet Ski, facing the utility box. 'Son,' Mike asked, 'what are you doing? Don't you remember what just happened?'

"Montana sucked in a deep breath of air as if to muster all the courage he could find, looked directly into Mike's eyes, and said, 'I can do this, Dad!'

"So, while Mike stood nearby, Montana took one giant step, a bigger step than he'd ever taken in his five-year-old life. And he made it! What a celebration took place as one courageous little boy and his proud dad gave each other high fives and hugs.

"Overcoming worry about having perfect performance, as well as conquering other worries and fears, may require steady determination and a step of faith that's well outside your comfort zone. But you can do it. Just look into the face of your heavenly Father and say, 'I can do this. I can trust you to use me just as I am.'"

In the five seconds it took for me to walk from the podium to the front row, I made a new resolution. No longer would I fret over my flaws and blunders. Seems at this stage of life mistakes are inevitable anyway, and they actually make others feel comfortable and free.

In a flash, I pictured my precious grandchild standing straight and tall on the brink of what must have seemed to him a giant chasm. I saw his determined look and felt his surge of self-confidence. I too had crossed a chasm of sorts. I'd moved from my old life into a new one and from an old way of thinking into a fresh, freeing viewpoint. Wiping a tear, I whispered, "I can do this, Father. Even if I don't do it perfectly."

If you are living in the second half of life, my guess is you've had your own share of mistakes and foibles to deal with. Seems that just when we reach the age at which we should be reverenced for our great wisdom, we lose all ability to communicate. Most of us stumble around making half sen-

20 GREAT THINGS ABOUT GETTING OLDER

1. It doesn't take so long for summer to come again.
2. You don't worry about which way hemlines are going.
3. Gray hair has more body.
4. The therapy is starting to kick in.
5. You can correct others without fear of being corrected yourself.
6. No one questions you if you take a sick day.
7. People pick up the things you drop.
8. People get out of the way when you drive down the street.
9. You have more and more chances to meet attractive doctors.
10. You own antiques after all.
11. Your spouse still snores, but now you can't hear it.
12. You can't regret what you can't remember.
13. Efferdent is good for cleaning jewelry too.
14. Spill all you like! You won't be punished.
15. Saying you forgot is enough of an excuse.
16. If you don't like the movie, you can go to sleep.
17. Mean old ladies yell with you, not at you.
18. Sagging jowls have made your cheekbones more prominent.
19. A flight attendant will help you put your bag in the overhead compartment.
20. You can tell your friends the same joke over and over and over.[2]

tences and forget really important things like the names of our own children. In fact, just the other day, as my husband, Joe, finished my sentence for me, I had to admit, "We've finally reached the age when it takes two people to make one sentence."

127

Nevertheless, our slightly confused generation has a lot of insight and some really strong opinions the world needs to hear. So let's gather our wits about us and keep spreading our well-seasoned wisdom—to everybody who has enough patience to listen.

10

If Only I Could Remember My Ginkgo

Coping with Memory Blips

I'm not losing my memory, it's just that my forgetterer is
highly advanced.

Jeanette Clift George

One day my friend Rebecca was speaking to a large
group of women at a Christian conference. "I'll
never forget the words my grandma wrote in the
front of her Bible," she began enthusiastically. As all eyes
and ears became acutely focused on my friend, her mind
suddenly went blank. Rebecca shifted from one foot to the
other and grinned nervously as the wheels of her mind
spun crazily without gaining any traction at all. Finally she
shrugged her shoulders and said, "Well, I can't remember
the words right now, but they did change my life."

I've noticed that among my circle of friends such episodes of memory loss are occurring much more frequently now that we are moving into the second half of life. One day Carolyn, one of my cronies, and I were standing in my kitchen chatting about a dear, mutual acquaintance—a gal we'd both known for more than twenty years. When I started to say her name, I blanked out. Carolyn was no help. We glared at each other with wide-eyed, blank expressions that are becoming all too familiar. Carolyn's gaze then shifted to a magnet stuck on my refrigerator, and she chuckled. She directed my attention to the adage. In bold letters it read: "It's hard to be nostalgic when you can't remember anything."

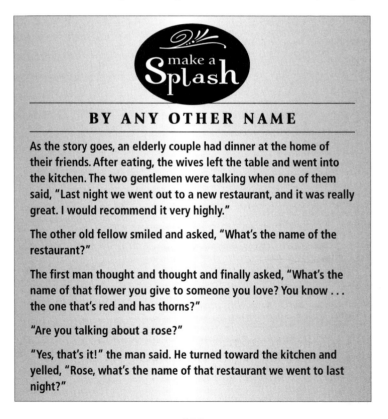

make a Splash

BY ANY OTHER NAME

As the story goes, an elderly couple had dinner at the home of their friends. After eating, the wives left the table and went into the kitchen. The two gentlemen were talking when one of them said, "Last night we went out to a new restaurant, and it was really great. I would recommend it very highly."

The other old fellow smiled and asked, "What's the name of the restaurant?"

The first man thought and thought and finally asked, "What's the name of that flower you give to someone you love? You know . . . the one that's red and has thorns?"

"Are you talking about a rose?"

"Yes, that's it!" the man said. He turned toward the kitchen and yelled, "Rose, what's the name of that restaurant we went to last night?"

Speaking of nostalgia, I have a hard time remembering which movies I've already seen. Surely I am not alone in this. For example, one day Joe and I were wandering through Blockbuster Video. I selected a new release and headed toward the cash register. I was standing in line with my pick in hand when Joe stepped behind me, leaned close to my ear, and whispered, "You've already seen it."

"Hmmm!" I mused. "Did I like it?"

"Yep! We watched it together. Don't you remember?"

Then he reminded me of one of the movie's classic lines. I had to admit that I'd done it again. I slipped my arm through his, whirled around, and announced just loud enough for those in line to hear, "I'm sorry, honey, I didn't realize you had already seen this! Let's pick something that we both haven't seen yet." Joe rolled his eyes and kept close tabs on me, serving as my portable memory until we found a movie I hadn't previously viewed.

I should have known to check with Joe before making a video selection. After all, he's our family expert in things theatrical. Ever since he was a carrot-topped, freckle-faced kid helping his dad run the projectors at Sweetwater's Texas Theatre, he's been able to name the flick, identify the stars, and provide several tidbits of trivia for most of the movies Hollywood has produced. On any given day, Joe may not remember what he had for breakfast, but he would never forget which movies he has seen. I have to admit, his expertise comes in handy.

My sister Lois understands my limitations. She recently told me she is rereading her huge stash of books. "I might as well save some money; I can't remember what I've read anyway," she quipped as she sipped coffee from her favorite mug. I couldn't hold back a burst of laughter when I read the bold print on the cup: "At my age, I've seen it all, heard it all, and done it all. I just can't remember it all."

If you are reading these words, are over fifty, and don't need help selecting a movie or a book, my guess is that you may be suffering from some other form of memory loss. I hate owning up to it, but sometimes I forget some really important stuff, like where I put my keys or billfold.

One such experience occurred while writing this book. (I just hate it when I have to experience my stories, though I must confess that after the trauma wears off, I can usually see the humor in them.) Anyway, when I find myself in a "stuck" place and am picking lint off the couch rather than writing a riveting chapter or two, I go elsewhere to write. I take a legal pad and visit Grapevine's botanical garden or a nearby park, coffee shop, or restaurant. Sometimes I go to Town Square in Southlake and sit by the fountain or near the gazebo. A change of scenery seems to get the creative juices flowing again. Besides, sometimes it feels good to sit in a public place and ignore people.

On this particular day, I grabbed my purse, pen, and pad and headed to Abuelo's, my favorite restaurant. Their unique blend of Tex-Mex and traditional Mexican food is guaranteed to soothe the nerves, lift depression, and jolt the memory. I ordered a luncheon special and dove into a basket of chips and salsa, and suddenly I was hit with a wave of inspiration. Between nibbles and dips, I wrote several pages of really good stuff, if I may say so myself (and I guess I just did). Unfortunately, it wasn't until I had completely finished my lunch, closed my portfolio, and started fumbling for my wallet that the memory-jolting properties of the meal kicked in. In my mind's eye I could see my little, brown leather wallet resting comfortably on my desk at home. I had no money, no credit card, and let's face it—no sense!

My heart pounded when the waiter came by. "Would you care for dessert?" he asked jovially.

"No, thank you," I answered, stifling an impulse to add, "Would you care to pay for my meal?" Instead, I ordered coffee. That should keep him busy for a while, I thought, pleased that my quick-thinking stall tactics were still in good working order. When he headed toward the kitchen, I dumped the contents of my purse on the table. I always keep an extra twenty stuffed in a side pocket for "such a time as this." (Okay, so this was not the first time "such" had happened!) Unfortunately, there was no money tucked away. Nothing. Nada. Zip. Then I remembered slipping my stash into a birthday card for our son Jason just a few days earlier. "If only I hadn't been so thoughtful, I wouldn't be in this mess!" I grumbled, my mood clearly deteriorating.

When the waiter returned, I changed my mind about dessert, ordering Death by Chocolate. If I was going to have to face the music, I figured I might as well try to get some endorphins flowing to ease the pain. As I savored the rich velvety sauce-drenched cake, I became Revived by Chocolate and came up with a plan. I located my cell phone and called Joe at work. "Honey," I began in my most seductive tone, "I'm just wondering if you'd like to join me for . . . dessert?"

"Now?" he replied, sounding utterly confused. "Gracie, it's 2:30. What's up?"

The gig was up. "Well, I did it again," I stammered with resignation. Then I launched into a detailed explanation until he sighed deeply and interrupted. "I'll be there as soon as I can." I felt like Lucy Ricardo as I took miniscule bites of cake and tiny sips of coffee, trying to nonchalantly pass the half hour it would take for Joe to make the drive. All the while, the waiter circled, eyeing me suspiciously. Before long my good-natured husband came to my rescue, and I slunk back to my car, feeling a few chips short of a full basket. The next day I tucked a twenty in the glove compartment of my SUV and stuck another in the secret compartment of my purse. Then I breathed a little prayer: "Lord, puhleeeze help me to remember where I put that money."

Most of us will suffer at least mild forms of memory loss during our golden years, and on most days we'll be able to laugh at ourselves. Still, there may come a time when we will have more withdrawals than deposits in our memory banks. But if we look closely, we may find some benefit even then. Isn't that what God promises?[1]

Consider the case of my beloved, ninety-four-year-old mother, who lives in an assisted living facility. Sometimes she's lucid and alert, quite able to carry on a relevant conversation. At times her old personality breaks through, providing much-needed comic relief to a complicated condition. For example, one day I was pushing her in her wheelchair from the dining room back to her quarters, and she glanced up at the decorative collage on the wall. The arrangement included a rolling pin, a galvanized pan, and an antique, corrugated washboard. She pointed one gnarled finger at the display and quipped, "That makes my back hurt!"

There are other times when Mom seems to disconnect. She becomes quiet, and when the family gathers in her room, she seems confused by the buzz of conversation. Sadly she has forgotten a huge part of her life, even some really significant things. The other day I stopped by to see her, as I do regularly. When I entered the room, she turned around and said, "How in the world did you find me?"

"Mother, I always know where you are," I answered. "You're not trying to hide from me, are you?"

She laughed happily and shook her head no. Then she pointed out the window. "I've been watching that worm.

The sidewalk is hot, and the poor guy can't seem to keep his tummy off the cement." I put my arms around her shoulders, and together we watched the worm wiggle and squirm until he made it to the cool moist soil on the other side of the walkway. As I plopped in her recliner, the thought occurred to me that the last time I had enjoyed something as simple and as wonderful as a worm was when my boys were little. Those were the days of discovering the joys of tadpoles, fireflies, and bugs. Yep, there is something refreshing about living in the present tense, waking up every day with a new start. My mother doesn't wonder about who came to see her yesterday or worry about what might happen tomorrow. Every visitor is celebrated like a reunion with a long-lost love, and the simplest things of life bring her great joy.

Still, there are many aspects of Mother's condition that trouble me. There is part of me that wants her to remember all my visits, all our loving and fun-filled conversations, and everything I do for her. But when I think about it entirely from her perspective, removing my desires from the equation, I realize memory loss can actually be a blessing. For one thing, as long as my mother is in this state of mind, my visits will never be considered routine or dull.

Another good thing is that folks like my mom forget painful memories as well as the good ones. In fact, at least in her case, the painful memories have been the first to go. For one thing, she doesn't remember her mother's funeral. It's a memory that's etched in my mind forever. (Okay, at least for now!) I sat beside my eighty-six-year-old mom as we witnessed the burial of her one-hundred-three-year-old mother. I remember helping Mom keep her coat closed when a cold breeze made the tent flaps pop and freezing rain pelted the canvas overhead. My mother's selective memory chooses to focus on her mother as if she were still with us. She enjoys talking about the pretty dresses Mama sewed for her children and the home-cooked meals she prepared while they worked in the fields.

Mother also forgets her own experiences of suffering. Last year her wheelchair scooted from under her, tossing her right out of her seat and onto the floor, face first. The accident caused a huge black eye, a small cut in her forehead, multiple bruises, and a sprained wrist. For several days my siblings and I hovered close by, watching over our mother carefully, worried that a blood clot might develop or that her elevated blood pressure might soar out of control. Mother talked about the experience for a few days, especially about the embarrassing black eye. Then the memories faded. After a couple of weeks the troubling thoughts were completely gone, leaving her carefree and happy as she wheeled down the halls once again. If the memory had lingered, the fear would have too, making her trips to the dining room something to be dreaded and feared. So it's good that she quickly forgot that awful fall.

Sometimes I think that losing some memories is part of our preparation for living in a place that's completely trouble free. Perhaps such loss helps us to mentally let go and move into another realm where there will be no more tears. Still, there are times when forgetfulness frustrates and complicates our second half of life here on planet Earth.

On our son Mike's birthday (the Big Four Oh!) we planned to cook dinner on his new grill—a birthday present from his wife, Jeanna. Joe and I decided we'd furnish the steaks, potatoes, and fresh corn on the cob. Before we went shopping, Jeanna helped us make a thorough grocery list. (As if we might forget something important!) Then we located my purse and keys and headed for the door.

"Now, here's how you go." Jeanna stood in front of us, being sure to make eye contact. "First, take a right." She twisted her tiny frame to the right and signaled a forward movement with her hands. "Turn left on Gosling." She turned her body that direction. Extending her arm in front of her, she said, "Now go through the first traffic light and keep going until you cross Woodland Lake." She took several baby steps forward so we'd get the picture. "You'll see the fire station on the left. Get over, like this." She took two sidesteps. "And turn into the shopping center. Right in front of you will be Pasta, Inc. Drive past that, over a couple of speed bumps, and you're at Kroger's." She smiled sweetly and asked, "Got it?"

Now I know we've gotten lost every single time we've visited them in the Woodlands. Still, I felt like a kindergartener getting directions for my first solo trip from the front door to my class. Just so I would appear grown-up, I rattled off what she'd just said. "Sure! Right leaving the neighborhood, left on Gosling, through the light, over the bridge, past the fire station, left into the shopping center, past Pasta Inc., onward to Kroger's."

"That's it!" She seemed surprised at how easy it sounded. "Now," she said, pushing a handful of papers into my hand, "here's the list. This is my Kroger's card, and this card gets points for Montana's school. Just show it to the checker."

I shoved the papers into my purse, and Joe and I headed for the door.

But before we could leave, Jeanna had one more thing on her mind. She must have hated to ask but felt it necessary. "Now, do either of you need to go potty?"

137

DOES ANYBODY CARE
LIKE MEDICARE?

Thought I'd let my doctor check me, 'cause I didn't feel quite right.

All those aches and pains annoyed me, and I couldn't sleep at night.

He could find no real disorder, but he wouldn't let it rest.

Since I was covered by insurance, we would do a couple tests.

To the hospital he sent me, though I didn't feel that bad.

He arranged for them to give me every test that could be had.

I was fluoroscoped and cystoscoped, my aging frame displayed

Stripped, on an ice-cold table, while my gizzards were x-rayed.

I was checked for worms and parasites, for fungus and the crud,

While they pierced me with long needles, taking samples of my blood.

Doctors came to check me over, probed and pushed and poked around,

And to make sure I was living, they then wired me for sound.

They have finally concluded (their results have filled a page)

They really couldn't help me, my affliction is old age.[2]

If you're anything like me and my absentminded buddies, you are probably more than a little concerned that you are losing your mind piece by piece. Well, take heart! I have some good news (if only I can remember where I filed it). Oh yes, here it is, right where I left it—stuck to my computer on a sticky note.

The good news is this: experts claim most of us will still be able to communicate in full sentences till the end of our days. It really depends on how we exercise the brain cells the Lord gave us. Learning new things, reading, and taking up hobbies will help keep the brain active and strong for the long haul.[3] Of course, we will all have occasional blips and blunders. Such temporary memory glitches are actually a trait common to all humanity—including our younger counterparts.

As we deal with our mental lapses and misfiring synapses, the most important thing is to have the right, positive attitude. And according to said experts, attitude is the thing that sets us apart from the forgetterers of the younger generation. While we worry and fret about our minds heading south, the thirty-something mind-set is to blame the problem on somebody else. So why not adopt a few of their coping skills? Next time you forget where you parked your car or left your keys, instead of thinking, *I'm an immediate candidate for the loony bin,* just stomp your feet and yell, "Who took my keys?"

11

The Bite of the Sandwich Generation

HANDLING MULTIGENERATIONAL MESSES

Listen to your life. See it for the fathomless mystery that it is.
In the boredom and pain of it no less than in the excitement and gladness:
touch, taste, smell your way to the holy and hidden heart of it because in the last analysis all moments are key moments, and life itself is grace.

Frederick Buechner

One Monday morning the phone rang persistently. When I answered, I recognized the voice of Birdie, the nurse at the assisted living facility where my mom recently took up residence. "Gracie," she began, "Your mother doesn't like her new wheelchair."

"What new wheelchair?"

"The motorized one. They delivered it last Friday and picked up her manual version today." Birdie paused and then added, "Your mother is in a real tizzy. Not only does she not *like* this chair, she's scared spitless. Says it goes too fast. Since she won't even sit in the new chair, she has no way to get to the dining room, and . . ."

"I'll be right there!"

I moaned as I gathered my purse and keys and headed out the door. On the way I wondered how in the world my mom, abiding in a one-room efficiency in a well-monitored unit, was able to select and purchase such a luxury item. And I had to marvel at the ingenuity of salespeople, especially those who represent certain home health groups. Seems they always have some newfangled gadget to make life easier for our nation's senior citizens. This wasn't the first time my mother had signed on the dotted line for supplies or medical treatments that I, the one with medical power of attorney as well as Mom's checkbook, had not deemed necessary.

Arriving at the residence, I parked my car and burst through the doors in a royal snit. "My mother *does not* have the authority to purchase medical equipment," I carped as I brushed past the receptionist, rounded the corner, and headed down the hall to Mom's room. Entering her door, I spotted my mother's latest purchase. The bright apple red scooter, parked smack in the middle of the room, sparkled in the light beaming from the overhead fixture. My mom sat slumped in her recliner with a sheepish look on her face.

"I don't want that thing!" she said. "And I don't know who ordered it. I want my old wheelchair back."

I patted Mom on the leg, then zeroed in on the snazzy chair. *Hmmm*, I thought, *I wonder how this contraption works.* I sank into the comfy leather seat and pushed the toggle switch mounted on the armrest. The scooter hummed as it inched forward. I nudged the switch to the left, and the chair pivoted that direction. I held the switch down hard and did a couple of doughnuts.

"Mom," I began in an upbeat tone, "this is cool! Maybe you *could* learn to use it!"

Mother shrugged her shoulders and grinned as she pushed herself out of her recliner and stumbled toward the chair. I showed her how to use the switch, got her started, and walked alongside as she drove in slow motion down the long hallway to the dining room. Mom successfully rounded the corner and headed toward her usual place. Unfortunately, she couldn't maneuver the contraption well enough to park it at the table. So I, being the mentally competent one, decided to take over the controls.

But when I moved the adjustable armrest out of the way, I must have switched the gears into high. For as soon as I pushed the switch forward, the chair took off at jackrabbit speed, ran over my foot, and slammed into the table, spilling iced tea and making everybody whoop.

I yelled.

The ladies sitting at the table rolled their eyes. (Thankfully, my mom's hearing aid batteries were weak. She just looked at me and smiled that beatific smile of hers.)

I cleaned up the tea, tucked a napkin in my mother's lap, and limped back to her room where I made three phone calls to my brothers and sisters and two appointments with administrators. The home health agency promised to pick up the motorized chair and return my mother's antique version the very next day.

Eventually I got Mom back to her room and into her recliner. Then I located my purse and headed back home.

Unfortunately, the wheelchair incident is only one of a number of emergency calls I've received. One recent Monday morning a similar SOS was sent my way. "Gracie," the receptionist chirped, "your mom is pretty upset today. She has lost her glasses, and we can't seem to find them. Last time she remembers having them was on Friday when she went to the beauty shop."

I couldn't believe my ears! My mom, who has worn glasses for the last forty years of her life, had been sitting around in a literal fog for three whole days. I jumped in my car and took off.

When I arrived I headed straight for the beauty shop. The beautician was out to lunch—apparently in more ways than one! As I searched the drawers and cabinet shelves for my mom's missing glasses, I overheard the small talk from the oldsters seated in the nearby living room. "Something's wrong with my eyes," one of them spoke up a little too loudly. (I couldn't help but grin as I thought, *Yep, and there's something wrong with your ears as well!*) Another resident with tight little curls in her silver hair staggered into the room just as I exited the beauty shop. "These are not mine," she yelled. She was holding on to her walker with her right hand and twirling a pair of bifocals with her left. As I headed onward to Mom's room, I thought, *We've got a really big problem here.* Seems the beautician had gotten everybody's glasses mixed up and the residents were bouncing off the walls—literally.

When I asked Mom what happened, she simply smiled, shrugged her shoulders, and claimed, "Somebody took them right off my face." After consoling her and doing a thorough search of her room, I proceeded to visit nearby residents. Cindy, the receptionist, helped. It was a puzzle that would not be solved right away. In fact, I had to leave before the staff untangled the mess. When I returned the next day, lo and behold, my mother was sitting in the living room chatting with her cronies. The right pair of glasses were perched on her nose, and she was wearing her typical smile. "Somebody just walked into my room and put them back on my face." She turned her palms up and shrugged her shoulders.

As I climbed into my car and began the thirty-mile drive toward home, I breathed a prayer for my precious mother. Then I remembered something important. I had to stop at Bath and Body Works before I got home. My two precious granddaughters, Mary Catherine and Abby, were coming for a sleepover, and I was completely out of bubble bath.

The competing events of the aforementioned day are typical of those that square off against each other regularly as I am "sandwiched" between being part-time caregiver for my mom and part-time playmate to my growing brood of grandchildren. Actually, I am more than a member of the sandwich generation; I'm part of something bigger—the club sandwich generation! My involvement with our three sons and two daughters-in-law adds another layer of bread and quite a bit of extra filling to the sandwiched days of my life.

Some of you may be sandwiched in a triple-decker that includes your children, parents, and grandparents. Others may be part of a group of grandmothers (a whopping 4.5 million of them![1]) who are helping to raise their children's children. Many of these grandparents have adult children living with them as well, and they are also taking care of their aging parents. I recently learned that more than twenty-two million working Americans are either totally responsible for or actively involved in caring for their elders.[2] That simply means there's a lot of overworked women in America's families who are not only holding down a job outside the home but also running errands, chauffeuring kids, keeping appointments, and taking care of their parents' basic needs.

THE NAME GAME

Several residents in a nursing home were lounging in the living room when an outgoing lady pushed through the front door and began greeting those seated nearby. She made her way around the circle and zeroed in on one gal she apparently recognized and knew.

The visitor went on and on, making small talk with the woman— seemingly oblivious all the while to the blank expression on the resident's upturned face. Finally she caught on that this resident didn't recognize her, so she leaned close so the old gal could get a good look. Then she smiled broadly and asked, "Do you know who I am?"

It was then that a little lady sitting in a wheelchair nearby interrupted, pointing her bony finger toward the nurse's station. "See that woman sitting there at that desk? If you ask her, she can tell you who you are."

Knowing that we are not alone in our task offers at least some consolation to members of the sandwich generation as we literally bite off more than we can chew day after day.

Such demanding schedules are especially daunting for those of us who are beginning to feel the effects of aging ourselves. As I'm easing into the AARP years, I find my energy level diminishing and aches and pains increasing, especially after a long day caring for my mother. In fact, I told my hubby the other day that there are times I feel not only "sandwiched" but tossed on the grill and toasted on both sides. Still, I manage to find a bit of humor as I scoot through the days of my life.

One evening shortly after a long day at Mom's apartment, I called our youngest son, Jason. He's the one I can usually count on to be understanding and supportive. I went into great detail as I described the events of that day, including my state of near exhaustion when I finally got home. "You know, Jason," I whined, "I honestly don't think I'll have anybody to do all this for me when I reach ninety-four!"

"Oh, Mom," Jason began in a serious tone, "don't worry about it. We'll take care of you. We'll put you in a nursing home and give you lots of drugs. That way, you'll be happy and we can say, 'She smiles all the time and sleeps like a baby.'"

I laughed shamelessly at my gregarious son, thankful for the good medicine laughter provides. For members of our fun-loving family, a good belly laugh is a coping mechanism that helps us handle even the most difficult situations—like those days when, in addition to fatigue, I'm emotionally worn out as well.

One day was particularly stressful. While I puttered around her room—cleaning, rearranging her clothes, serving coffee and cookies—Mom talked incessantly, saying the same things over and over again. Usually I take such rote conversation in stride, but on this day her repeated questions and stories were getting to me.

How can people call this stage a second childhood? While there may be some similarities, there are major differences. A mother toils, teaches, and faces some of the same challenges with her children, but she's rewarded by seeing new growth. With the roles reversed—when children assume the role of "parent" to their parents—there is only loss. It hurts to watch my mother's personality fade like a beautiful flower that curls inward when it's past its bloom. Sometimes my only reward is my mother's sweet smile and a mischievous twinkle in

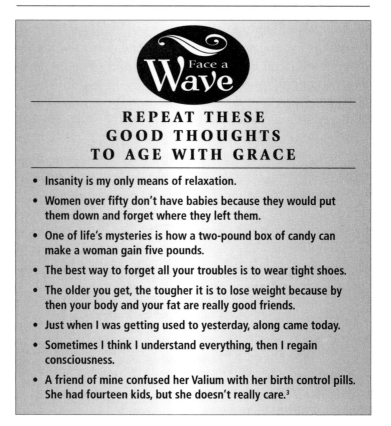

Face a Wave

REPEAT THESE GOOD THOUGHTS TO AGE WITH GRACE

- Insanity is my only means of relaxation.
- Women over fifty don't have babies because they would put them down and forget where they left them.
- One of life's mysteries is how a two-pound box of candy can make a woman gain five pounds.
- The best way to forget all your troubles is to wear tight shoes.
- The older you get, the tougher it is to lose weight because by then your body and your fat are really good friends.
- Just when I was getting used to yesterday, along came today.
- Sometimes I think I understand everything, then I regain consciousness.
- A friend of mine confused her Valium with her birth control pills. She had fourteen kids, but she doesn't really care.[3]

her eye. And in spite of our limitations, it's nothing short of amazing how the two of us can get ourselves into some jam or perplexing situation that makes us both giggle.

For example, one day when I dropped in on Mom, she wasn't wearing a bra. "Mom," I began, "You look a little droopy this morning. Did you forget something important?"

"Nope," she answered, "I didn't forget! I just got to thinking. I've worn a bra for over eighty years. I'm not going to wear one anymore."

Now, I've got just one thing to say about that. You go, girl!

148

PART 4

Diving into Middle-Age Crazies

12

Keeping Both Oars in the Water

REFUSING TO BE OUTPACED BY TECHNOLOGY

Some people say you can't teach an old dog new tricks.
I've just got one thing to say about that: you are not an old
dog!

Dr. Jay Adams

I live in a family of men—including one husband, three sons, and four grandsons. And each and every one of them is a geek. Oh, I don't mean that they have greasy hair and wear their pants pulled up to their armpits—I'm talking about computer geeks. This crew is not only computer literate, they're obsessed. I dare say even addicted. They work with computers; their hobbies are computer related (digital cameras, webcams, and a program called Photoshop); they play computer games and converse with each other via electronic mail. Incidentally, my two granddaughters are computer savvy as well but so far have managed to keep their "compu-habit" well under control. Not so with their compulsive grandpa!

My husband went through a period of time when he would come home from work, head directly to our study, log on to the Web, and surf until bedtime. You know the score. You've got your Fishing Widow, your Golf Widow, and the widow of the new millennium—the Computer Widow. I walked in the study one evening just in time to see Joe polishing the screen of his new monitor with a Windex towelette. When he saw me standing behind him with my hands on my hips, he whispered sweetly to the machine, "There now, let's clean that dirty face of yours and make it nice and shiny."

"That's it, Joe!" I blurted out in my solitary frustration. "How about trading that Windex for a bottle of lotion and come give me a shoulder rub?" I turned on my heels and headed down the hall.

From that point on, I referred to the family computer as "Wife." I could tell the term of nonendearment made my hubby a bit uncomfortable, but not enough to slow him down or make him consider joining a twelve-step program for compu-holics. Eventually I learned to laugh about my husband's "first love," consoling myself that at least his addiction kept him home where I could make sure he wasn't getting into trouble.

Besides, I began to realize that there were certain perks associated with having computer smarts. For one thing, our family had never been closer. Even though the communication between our sons and their dad was handled by an Instant Messenger instead of the postman, and even though words weren't being exchanged over the telephone verbally, we knew more about what our kids were doing than we'd ever known during precomputer years. Of course, I needed Joe to translate and interpret the abbreviations, numerical codes, and nonwords these guys used to communicate with each other. I remember one time in particular when their interaction left me scratching my graying head in utter confusion.

Our oldest son, Matt, had joined us for dinner. Afterward, as we lounged in the living room, the conversation between him and his dad took its inevitable turn toward their home computers.

"Dad," Matt said, "how's your Pentium running?"

"Doing great!" Joe responded with pride, as if he were talking about a prized sports car. He had upgraded and couldn't help working in a bit of bragging. "How 'bout you? Did you get that 2.5 gigabyte chip like I recommended?"

"No, I spent my money on a high-speed modem."

"DSL or cable?"

"DSL," Matt answered. "Sure feels good to get rid of that old 56K baud modem."

"Well, I can top that! I got an 80 gig hard drive the other day." Joe paused, relishing the envy on Matt's face, and then added, "And . . . WIN XP Professional."

Matt quickly countered, "But do you have enough memory to run XP?"

"I've got 512 megabytes!"

"Wow!" Matt was clearly impressed. Still, I thought I detected a small sense of resignation as the young whippersnapper realized he had been out-computered by an old pro.

As for me, I sat dumfounded! I'd heard every bit of the guys' conversation but didn't understand a thing they'd said. To this point in my life, a "chip" was a nifty edible tool with which one could scoop up cheese dip. And "bite" was something involving teeth, dentures, or a mosquito. I could only imagine what "baud" meant. I figured it was the proper English way to describe a terrible, awful, really bad day. It was more than bad; it was "baud."

No matter that I'm left in the dark when it comes to interpreting Geek-ese. As the evening wound down, there was no mistaking the underlying message of the interchange between father and son. As Matt stood to leave, he put his arms around his dad's shoulders and said, "Hey, I really love you, Dad!"

Our son Mike is into technology with the same gusto as his older brother. He computes for an oil company in The Woodlands and plays with his laptop when he gets home. Last year at Christmas, we bought him a wireless router. (For you novices: Joe explained to me that it's a device to make Mike's laptop and his desktop computers work in tandem—without wires no less.) Even though I failed to see the value in such a cozy arrangement, Mike was ecstatic. I was flabbergasted as I watched him gush and salivate over that powder-blue and black plastic box with flashing lights mounted on top. For two days afterward, as my daughter-in-law Jeanna and I puttered around the house enjoying our more traditional gifts, Mike and Joe fondled the new hardware and engaged in fluent compu-talk.

While I am just learning to speak the same language as the men in my family, I realize that it comes naturally to members of the younger generation. In fact, it seems to be the first language for many of our kids—even five-year-old kindergarteners.

My friend Judy, a kindergarten teacher at Colleyville's Glenhope School, was working her way through a "Concepts of Print" assessment at the beginning of the year. Her students sat in a circle. Judy pointed to the different forms of punctuation and asked the children to identify them. First she pointed out the question mark, then an exclamation point, and then a comma. The children explained the function of each. Finally she pointed to a period and asked, "Now, what does this mean?"

A cute little blond, blue-eyed girl waved her hand in the air. "I know, I know," she shouted. "It means dot com."

Even preschoolers know the lingo well. Four-year-old Jordan, son of my friend Dena, was playing games on his computer while his grandpa looked over his shoulder. The

KEEPING IN TOUCH

Mabel, a charming, techno-savvy woman in her sixties, decided to purchase a new pager. The device came complete with a clip so she could attach it to her belt. She was no sooner out of the store and seated in her car than she installed two batteries and got herself hooked up and ready. Now her family and co-workers could reach her at any time, any place. Thing is, nobody tried to reach her that afternoon.

When she got home, she unclipped the gadget and put it on her desk with her purse and keys. The next morning she put it back on. By that evening, she had not received a single message. She complained to her friend Ethel, "I guess I didn't really need a pager after all. Not one person has beeped me."

Ethel leaned close to Mabel's waist so she could get a good look at the device clipped to her belt loop. "Well, no wonder," she chirped. "You're wearing your garage door opener."

older gentleman was mesmerized by the skills of his tiny grandson. "How in the world do you do that?" he asked.

Jordan simply answered, "Oh, I just click and dwag."

One day in a moment of quiet reflection, my thoughts turned to the predicament I found myself in when our youngest son, Jason, packed up his things and headed off to college. I had decided to pursue my dream of becoming a writer and had already learned by trial and a lot of error to peck out sentences using an old DOS program that Joe had installed for me. But I knew if I was going to produce an article that had a fighting chance of making the world a better place, I needed a bit of professional help—the kind of assistance that could only come from a well-informed association with (you guessed it) "Wife."

So I enrolled in a class at a nearby junior college, where I ended up taking three semesters of instruction and hands-on training to familiarize myself with the "other woman" in Joe's life. (Yeah, I know, life has a strange way of making you do things you swore you would never do.) Through the years my compu-skills have grown. I've learned how to format a disk and store information in separate files on my hard drive. Recently I worked my way completely through the manual for my spiffy new Bible study program. Still, I must confess I have a hard time staying afloat in the changing current of our high-tech culture.

For one thing, I'd like to have a PDA. I would buy myself one if I thought I could learn how to use it. You do know what a PDA is, don't you? It's a palm-sized digital assistant. The thought behind this gadget is that in a package no bigger than the palm of your hand, you can have your own personal assistant—a secretary in your pocket—to keep up with your schedule and handle your important data.

The problem is, before your personal assistant can go to work for you, she has to be programmed. And just the thought of that could send a woman like me into an all-out tizzy. When I see one of my children or grandchildren pecking on their PDA with that little pointy thing or notice one of my girlfriends squinting at the miniature screen, my eyes glaze over. It all seems so complicated.

Even though using a PDA has me mystified, I can at least use a cell phone. In fact, I've used one for many years. Joe gave me my first model—a huge contraption mounted in a brief case—as a Christmas present when cellular service was in its infant stages. It was not a luxury item, according to my hubby, since I had a bad reputation for getting lost or stranded in my car. We both felt safer with me having a connection to home. The tiny white cell phone that I carry today bears little resemblance to that first mobile unit. It's so darn cute, I just couldn't help but want to know it personally. I read its manual, programmed my frequently called numbers into its database, and created my own personal greeting and personalized ring ("Ode to Joy").

Now if I could just teach my brother Charles how to do all that!

Recently I was tooling down the highway when I got a call from him. "Gracie, are you all right?" he asked.

"Yep! Just fine," I answered. "Why are you asking?"

"Well, your name keeps showing up on my cell phone screen, like I've had a message from you, and I'm not sure if this is one you sent last week or if you called again today."

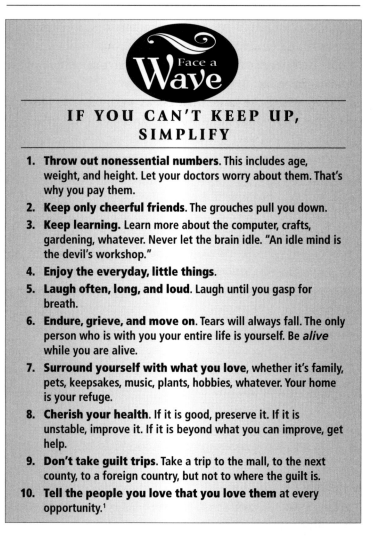

IF YOU CAN'T KEEP UP, SIMPLIFY

1. **Throw out nonessential numbers**. This includes age, weight, and height. Let your doctors worry about them. That's why you pay them.
2. **Keep only cheerful friends**. The grouches pull you down.
3. **Keep learning**. Learn more about the computer, crafts, gardening, whatever. Never let the brain idle. "An idle mind is the devil's workshop."
4. **Enjoy the everyday, little things**.
5. **Laugh often, long, and loud**. Laugh until you gasp for breath.
6. **Endure, grieve, and move on**. Tears will always fall. The only person who is with you your entire life is yourself. Be *alive* while you are alive.
7. **Surround yourself with what you love**, whether it's family, pets, keepsakes, music, plants, hobbies, whatever. Your home is your refuge.
8. **Cherish your health**. If it is good, preserve it. If it is unstable, improve it. If it is beyond what you can improve, get help.
9. **Don't take guilt trips**. Take a trip to the mall, to the next county, to a foreign country, but not to where the guilt is.
10. **Tell the people you love that you love them** at every opportunity.[1]

Charles cleared his throat and said, "I thought I deleted your last message, but, well, do you know how to do it?"

"Hmmm, every phone is different," I said, "so—"

"I've been reading my manual," Charles interrupted. "Let me get it." After a moment or two, I heard him thumbing through the pages. "I'm on page eighty-six!"

I burst out laughing at the thought of my brother (or any human being for that matter) plowing through almost a hundred pages of data and still not having a clue how to delete a message.

Recognizing the ludicrousness as well, Charles laughed with me, then paused and added, "You know what, Gracie? I don't want to know all this stuff. I just need a simple list of commands. You know, maybe with numbers or bullets . . ." His voice trailed off, and then he added, "I've just finished reading *Computers for Dummies*. I guess I need *Cell Phones for Dummies!*"

Charles and I laughed again, enjoying a moment of real connection—and I don't mean because we were using the same cellular space.

As I pushed the Off button on my phone and slipped it back into my purse, my mind returned to the time when I came to terms with my incompetence. "My name is Gracie and I'm technically inept."

As my technical faux pas set in, my mental gymnastics took a humorous twist. "I may be dumb, but I'm not stupid!" I announced to myself with all the confidence I could muster. Then as honesty began tugging at my sleeve, I conceded a little more of my self-respect. "Well, I may be stupid, but I'm not ignorant!" Then truth began to set me free, and pretty soon I was going all the way. "Oh well, I might as well be really honest. I'm a trinity of ineptitude—I'm dumb, I'm stupid, and I'm ignorant!" To admit being technologically challenged was no big deal. But to acknowledge a state of total incompetence caused me a measure of angst. There was nothing left for me to do but make an appointment with an advisor at that junior college and get with the program.

I'm sure there are some of you who identify with Charles and me. If so, perhaps it's time for you to purchase a few good books for dummies or enroll in a class for the computer illiterate. As the old saying goes, "Time's a wastin'!" And as the new saying goes, "Stop dwagging your feet!"

Now I am not suggesting that you have to enter into an intimate relationship with your technological toys—but you do need to at least begin courting.

13

We're in the Same Boat

UNTANGLING COMPLICATED RELATIONSHIPS

A friend is clothed with Seraphim wings, running ahead
   of me,
shouting, "holy, holy, holy," pushing me into the
   presence of God.
The spirit of Aaron and Hur clothe a friend. Running
   behind me,
she sits me on a rock, holds up my weary hands
and waits with me in silence while the Lord fights my battle.

Linda Dillow

It was almost time for lunch when I located my purse, keys, and notebook and headed out the door. I was going to meet my friends at one of our town's major tourist attractions—okay, our only tourist attraction—the bakery and tea room known as Mary of Puddin' Hill. For as long as I'd lived in Greenville, Texas (more than twenty-five years, mind you!), this was the place women gathered for soup and salad and the tastiest fruitcake morsels and gourmet chocolate on the face of God's green earth. (Actually, it's more like "God's black earth" around Greenville, for the soil is so dark and gooey that when it rains it reminds us all of, well . . . chocolate puddin'!)

When it comes to girlfriend gatherings, atmosphere is equally important as good food. And the surroundings at Puddin' Hill are delightful, with just the right balance of "cuteness" and antiquity. Our group had been meeting there long enough that the owner, Mary Lauderdale, and her daughter, Pud, always reserved a big table for us in the back room. We never quite figured out if that was for our convenience or for the comfort of her other customers, for we could be quite a boisterous gaggle of girls.

I guess, since we were a group of speakers and writers, one should expect us to be loud. It's in our genes! Still, it was nice to have a measure of privacy as we deliberated on future projects. Usually when we met in public, we were able to quiet ourselves enough to take care of a few items of business. I remember one morning in particular. Someone claimed that if we were going to be a writer's group with any recognition at all, we needed a name. You should have heard us discussing this important matter.

After batting around such lofty titles as the Greenville Writer's Guild, Fran, the quietest member of our group, suggested a name that made us bend double with the giggles. "Well, since we all have such a strong nurturing streak, and . . . since we're no longer a bunch of spring chickens," she said sweetly, "we could call ourselves Hens with Pens!" After that, the discussion got funnier by the minute, especially when another gal suggested Chicks with Bics! From that day on, we laughingly dubbed ourselves the Hens. We had no idea the label would ever be mentioned outside our group.

But, as they say in writer's circles, the rest of the story had not been written.

One day when we gathered for our regular meeting, one of the members came up with the most brilliant idea ever hatched by a mama "Hen." She cackled out loud and said, "We should write a book together!"

After that the ideas began to fly like down from a busted pillow, as each gal told what contribution she could make. We'd all reached the point in our lives where we had a nest full of experiences we couldn't wait to tell other hurting chicks. We wanted to encourage our readers to become more confident and to grow in courage as they faced the complicated issues of life. We'd read in prominent women's magazines and current books about how to develop confidence, and frankly, we disagreed with most of them! Our book would promote a healthy, Christ-centered view of self-esteem. We'd lived long enough to know that assertiveness or feminism is not enough to see a gal through complicated times. After we decided on a direction, we put our limited store of brain cells together and started discussing titles.

Eventually we decided to call our book *Courage for the Chicken Hearted*. It seemed the perfect title for a book written by a flock of Hens who, even though we'd lived half a lifetime, still sometimes struggled with feeling chicken about certain issues.

Throughout the next few months, we met regularly. We edited each other's work, made sure our stories fit together well, and encouraged each other to press on to complete the project. After sharing our stories with each other, laughing a lot, and sharing that wonderful chicken feed from Puddin' Hill, we almost always left with our confidence renewed. As an added blessing, incredible bonding took place.

We were not only united in one purpose—the writing project—but we were women who really loved each other. We opened up about our problems, sharing some of our disappointments and troubles. We loved each other through all sorts of crises, from newly emptied nests, to trouble with our chicks, to feeling as though the sky really, truly was falling. Sometimes we cried with each other. Always we prayed for each other.

Eventually, by putting our beaks together, we managed to peck out a book that God would bless.

But the most important thing that happened, at least for me, was what I learned in that group about friendship. Most of you probably have no desire to get involved in a complicated group venture like writing. But my guess is you're involved in some sort of group, team, or relationship that could use a bit of preening. Therefore, I make a not-so-chicken-hearted offer to share what I have learned. May the following thoughts help you feather your nest with a few new ideas to make your group projects fun and successful.

Perhaps the most important thing I learned is this: *Differences are something to celebrate, not simply tolerate.* Even though we loved each other dearly and still do to this day, the Hens did not always see things alike. In fact, the longer we worked together, the more obvious our differences became. These were not surface or petty issues. Instead, they seemed to come from a place deep within our souls. After doing a little research, the reason became obvious. Among the five of us, there were three distinct personality types and four different spiritual gifts. We were connected to four different churches of various denominations. No wonder we sometimes came to five different conclusions!

Occasionally, because of our distinctiveness, a few feathers got ruffled. At least once, a full-blown ruckus erupted in the hen house. We leaned heavily on the following words as we worked together: "Welcome with open arms fellow believers who don't see things the way you do. And don't jump all over them every time they do or say something you don't agree with—even when it seems that they are strong on opinions but weak in the faith department. Remember, they have their own history to deal with. Treat them gently."[1] Such grace freed us from tension and helped us appreciate each other.

Eventually I grasped another important concept: *Unique gifts and talents are given to complete, not compete.* The longer we worked together, the more we learned to appreciate our differences. We truly needed the diversity God had given us, and he used it to keep us balanced, to round out our perspectives. When one of us felt weak in a certain area, another Hen would come alongside and provide the strength needed. When one of us was confused (which was more often than we'd like to admit), another member of our flock seemed to have the answer.

It didn't take me long to understand how much we needed Rebecca to remind us to pause amid the busy planning and pray. We needed Fran to help us line things up like surgical instruments on a tray to remind us to be kind and sensitive to each other. We needed Susan's creativity, spontaneity, and lack of inhibition. We even needed Becky's free spirit and her sense of humor lest we take ourselves too seriously or think we had all the answers. And, of course, the group needed me . . . to keep things moving, to make sure all the bases were covered.

Most of us are drawn to people who are very different from us. We gravitate toward friends with opposite strengths. We like to be around people who've come from different backgrounds or who have complementary, but not exactly the same, personalities. Even though we know that "opposites

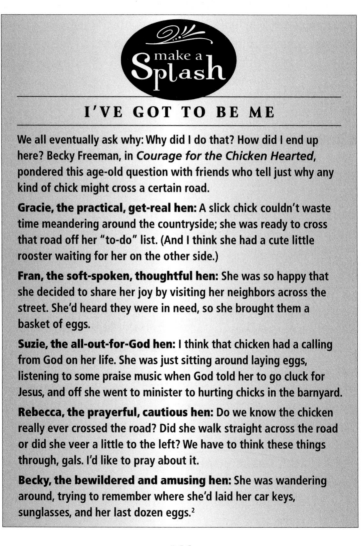

make a Splash

I'VE GOT TO BE ME

We all eventually ask why: Why did I do that? How did I end up here? Becky Freeman, in *Courage for the Chicken Hearted*, pondered this age-old question with friends who tell just why any kind of chick might cross a certain road.

Gracie, the practical, get-real hen: A slick chick couldn't waste time meandering around the countryside; she was ready to cross that road off her "to-do" list. (And I think she had a cute little rooster waiting for her on the other side.)

Fran, the soft-spoken, thoughtful hen: She was so happy that she decided to share her joy by visiting her neighbors across the street. She'd heard they were in need, so she brought them a basket of eggs.

Suzie, the all-out-for-God hen: I think that chicken had a calling from God on her life. She was just sitting around laying eggs, listening to some praise music when God told her to go cluck for Jesus, and off she went to minister to hurting chicks in the barnyard.

Rebecca, the prayerful, cautious hen: Do we know the chicken really ever crossed the road? Did she walk straight across the road or did she veer a little to the left? We have to think these things through, gals. I'd like to pray about it.

Becky, the bewildered and amusing hen: She was wandering around, trying to remember where she'd laid her car keys, sunglasses, and her last dozen eggs.[2]

attract," it seems we no sooner find a soul mate than we begin trying to change that person. There's something deep inside our chicken hearts that causes us to want our friends to be just like we are—to see things the way we do. But God had a purpose when he created us with unique gifts and talents.

He provided a word picture in Scripture—one that we can all understand—when he described his people as various parts of a human body. "You can easily enough see how this kind of thing works by looking no further than your own body. Your body has many parts—limbs, organs, cells—but no matter how many parts you can name, you're still one body."[3]

Our human bodies are a living, ever-present visual aid to help us develop better relationships. Next time you find yourself wanting everybody to do things your way, look at your hand and think of what it can accomplish when it works in harmony with your wrist, your arm muscles, your rotor cuff, and your shoulder.

The passage explains further: "A body isn't just a single part blown up into something huge. It's all the different-but-similar parts arranged and functioning together. If Foot said, 'I'm not elegant like Hand, embellished with rings; I guess I don't belong to this body,' would that make it so? If Ear said, 'I'm not beautiful like Eye, limpid and expressive; I don't deserve a place on the head,' would you want to remove it from the body? If the body was all eye, how could it hear? If all ear, how could it smell? As it is, we see that God has carefully placed each part of the body right where he wanted it."[4]

Picture a human body that's just one huge eyeball. How would that kind of body function? I guess if the whole body were one eye, we would all see things the same way. But what if somebody needed a helping hand? Why, all the body could do is . . . roll! God knew exactly what he was doing when he made us one body with many different parts. We need to stop trying to do corrective surgery on something that's just perfect.

Which brings me to perhaps the most important aspect of friendship: *God uses our friends to demonstrate the many facets of his goodness and compassion.* When a crisis comes, what would we do without our friends?

One morning, three weeks after back surgery, I became frustrated. I felt tired and weak. The six-inch incision in my lower back was swollen and tender. Since I was already taking antibiotics, I wondered why my back seemed infected. Sending an SOS heavenward, I cried, "Lord, please tell me what to do."

I didn't hear an audible voice, but immediately I knew exactly what to do. I called the doctor's office. "I want the doctor to check my back. May I come now?" I was surprised when the nurse answered yes.

When I arrived at the doctor's office, he examined me and suggested I check into the hospital. In fact, a nurse escorted me down the long hallway that led from the office suites into the hospital corridors. As soon as I settled into a room and changed into one of their gowns, techs came to take me downstairs for an MRI.

The test revealed pockets of infection spreading near my third vertebrae. The doctor would have to perform surgery again. When he said they would need to "wash out the wound," I cringed. I imagined the surgical team pulling a water hose through the swinging doors and power-washing my gaping incision. I breathed a prayer for the anesthesiologist: "Lord, please make sure he gives me enough of the right kind of medi-

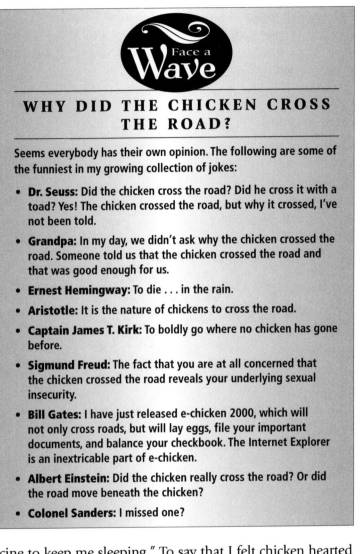

WHY DID THE CHICKEN CROSS THE ROAD?

Seems everybody has their own opinion. The following are some of the funniest in my growing collection of jokes:

- **Dr. Seuss:** Did the chicken cross the road? Did he cross it with a toad? Yes! The chicken crossed the road, but why it crossed, I've not been told.

- **Grandpa:** In my day, we didn't ask why the chicken crossed the road. Someone told us that the chicken crossed the road and that was good enough for us.

- **Ernest Hemingway:** To die . . . in the rain.

- **Aristotle:** It is the nature of chickens to cross the road.

- **Captain James T. Kirk:** To boldly go where no chicken has gone before.

- **Sigmund Freud:** The fact that you are at all concerned that the chicken crossed the road reveals your underlying sexual insecurity.

- **Bill Gates:** I have just released e-chicken 2000, which will not only cross roads, but will lay eggs, file your important documents, and balance your checkbook. The Internet Explorer is an inextricable part of e-chicken.

- **Albert Einstein:** Did the chicken really cross the road? Or did the road move beneath the chicken?

- **Colonel Sanders:** I missed one?

cine to keep me sleeping." To say that I felt chicken hearted would have been a gross understatement. I was downright scared.

But early the next morning, the Hens started hovering. One by one Becky, Fran, Rebecca, and Susan called to encourage me. They each ended their conversation with, "Gracie, may I pray for you?" It was not unusual that I'd hear from my friends, but it was a bit odd that every single one of them asked to pray for me.

My first thought was, *Gracie Girl, you are in a heap of trouble.*

My second thought was, *God has not forgotten you.* The fact that he had called my friends to prayer was a source of great comfort. And as we prayed together, with telephones pressed against our ears, the God of the universe reached down and touched me. The spiritual connection that came through the telephone lines gave me a new surge of energy and faith. In the words of Barbara Johnson, "I felt wrapped in God's comfort blanket of love."

Surgery went well, although the lab tests confirmed a serious infection. We had caught it in the early stages. The doctors knew exactly which antibiotics to use. For six weeks, twice a day, I would be hooked up to an IV to get the meds I needed.

The road to recovery would have its bumps and chuckholes, but our prayers had been answered. I would eventually be strutting around the barnyard once again, trying to take charge of the flock. In the meantime, the Hens continued to be messengers of God's love, providing an "eggstra" measure of courage to my chicken heart and leaving me with a nest full of precious memories.

14

Snow on the Rooftop and Fire in the Furnace

FANNING FLAMES
OF WELL-SEASONED LOVE

Grow old along with me!
The best is yet to be,
The last of life, for which the first was made;
Our times are in His hand
Who saith, "A whole I planned."
Youth shows but half; trust God; see all, nor be afraid!

Robert Browning

The blaring of a car's horn outside my study window startled me. I spun around in my chair, lifted one slat of the blind, and peered outside. A flaming-red Corvette roared into our driveway and screeched to a halt. Joe, my husband of forty-two years, was in the driver's seat. I must say he looked charming with his necktie blown over his shoulder and his white hair glistening in the sun. I slipped on my shoes and ran outside to see what was up. I soon learned he'd won an award at work.

For two years Joe, a retired IBM computer tech, had been working for our oldest son, Matt, in a growing new computer business—my baby's brainchild—which, I might add, was doing quite well. In fact, well enough to purchase a brand-new Corvette for the exclusive use of its high-performing employees. "It's an incentive," Matt had explained, "nudging our employees to do an even better job in the workplace." Apparently it worked, for the award was the company's most coveted.

It's important to mention at this point that the company's mascot is the wolf. For employees of this budding enterprise, the wolf symbolizes aggressiveness, teamwork, and cooperation. The company grants awards to its workers in keeping with their chosen mascot, including the Silver Wolf Award and the Leader of the Pack. Each month the racy vehicle goes to the pack leader, who gets to drive it for twenty-one days. The license plate on the car is framed in chrome, proclaiming in bold letters that the driver is the Leader of the Pack! The personalized license plate reads "B A WOLF."

Imagine two old codgers like Joe and me tooling around town in a sports car that's advertising the driver's status as "a wolf," encouraging the people driving behind us to B A WOLF! Now, I realize there are certain phrases that mean one thing to folks my age and something entirely different to members of the younger generation. But when Joe and I were the age of our son, it wasn't all that nice for a guy to be called a wolf. In fact, it was a rather derogatory appellation meaning a guy who was a big flirt. (Picture a young dude with long sideburns, sitting on the hood of his jalopy, whistling or making wolf calls at every girl who walks by.)

My hubby thought it funny to be dubbed a wolf. He loved getting to drive the car, and he couldn't wait to take me out for a howling good time. That night we made plans to take the car for a spin on the back roads near Fort Worth.

Early the next morning we climbed into the snazzy sports car. Well, actually, we didn't climb in—you climb into an SUV. To take a seat in a Corvette, you have to open the door, stand as close as possible to the black leather bucket seats, hold on to the top of the car, put one leg inside, pivot your body so that your buttocks enter the premises first, bend your knees slowly, and then drop in. (Getting out is another matter.)

Anyway, we got up early the next morning, dropped into the snazzy sports car, and backed out of our driveway. We were heading to our favorite restaurant—the one where the blue hair folks hang out. Now I refuse to consider myself part of the Blue Hair Gang, but I'm smart enough to realize that members of this generation are the casserole experts of the world. They definitely know where to find the best food in town. We whipped into the parking lot and parked the car. Joe managed to pry himself out of his seat and came around to my side to lend a helping hand.

When he opened the door, I glanced down at the black surface of the pavement, only six inches beneath where I sat. I turned toward my hubby and placed both feet squarely on the asphalt. In this position I could have rested my chin on my arthritic knees. I noticed a crowd gathering, and I wasn't about to appear as old or infirm as I felt. I smiled broadly and extended both hands in Joe's direction. He stepped backward and pulled. Before I knew it, I was in an upright position. Joe winked at me and patted me on the bottom. As we strolled toward the café, arm in arm, I couldn't resist saying, "You old wolf, you!"

IT'S AMAZING ALRIGHT!

Several gentlemen from the First Baptist Church visit a nearby nursing home regularly. The folks who reside there love to see the Baptists burst through the doors with their bright, smiling faces, carrying their guitars and sheet music.

The residents love to sing—especially the older hymns of the faith. And the best part of the sing-song is "request time." Their hands shoot up in the air like a bunch of schoolkids hoping for a chance to suggest their personal favorites. Even though many of the older folks deal with short-term memory loss, they never seem to forget the words of their favorite hymn.

One morning a lady requested "Amazing Grace." The group sang along without missing a beat—or a word—through all five stanzas.

But as soon as the guitarist strummed the last chord, an absent-minded but feisty little lady on the front row stuck her hand high in air and bellowed, "Now can we sing 'Amazing Grace'?"

After breakfast we headed south on a country road leading to Granbury, where we "put the pedal to the metal." All day we visited the quaint shops and antiques stores. Everywhere we went, people glared and grinned. I don't think I'd had so much fun since we were newlyweds, driving around the college campus in our '57 Chevy.

As we sank into the bucket seats and began heading back home, the life Joe and I had lived together began to play through my mind like reruns of *Ozzie and Harriet*. We'd had a good life, a blessed journey. We'd also sailed through our share of choppy waters and weathered a few major storms.

Through it all, we'd managed to keep the embers glowing in the furnace of our hearts.

Perhaps there are some of you reading this story who simply cannot relate. When you got married, you fully intended to live out your days with the "fire in your furnace" burning brightly. But somewhere along the way, the flame sputtered and went out, leaving the coals on the hearth of your life cold and gray. Maybe somebody broke up the fire or stomped it out or doused buckets of cold water on it until there was nothing left but charred broken pieces too wet to ever catch a spark again. But there are others of you who simply need to rekindle the flame by adding a bit of new wood or gathering some extra kindling or twigs. I am sympathetic with you no matter what your experiences have been, for life happens to all of us, and nobody knows better than me what it takes to keep the fire burning.

I remember one dark period in our life. We'd sailed through midlife crisis without hitting even one sandbar, only to find ourselves in turbulent seas when we faced our own unique version of the empty nest syndrome.

We had two sons, Matt and Mike, and then twelve years later another, Jason. We had no time for a midlife crisis—even if we had wanted one! We were too busy with high school football games and helping Matt and Mike prepare for SATs and find the right college, while at the same time attending Jason's little league games and kindergarten programs.

We put our relationship crisis on hold until our older two were on their own and our youngest was in those easy childhood years. It's a time when parenting is relatively stress free, kids think their mom and dad are "cool," and being seen with them is fun and not embarrassing at all. (This stage doesn't last long, but it's bliss personified while it does!)

Maybe Joe and I had too much time on our hands as we adjusted to our semi-empty nest. Whatever the reason, the embers on the hearth of our hearts were dying, mostly from neglect and lack of fresh fuel.

Joe began to fill his leisure time with hobbies and the latest computer software. When he got home from work, he'd head directly to our study, where he'd boot up the computer and surf the Web for hours on end. I spent most of my spare time in the living room reading, journaling, and doing creative writing projects. Jason retreated to his upstairs bedroom to do homework or entertain himself with his Hot Wheels and G.I. Joe collections. In our tri-level home, it was possible for us to live tri-level lives with very little connection to each other. How sad! Eventually we realized our marriage was in real trouble. I longed for the warmth and companionship I'd lost.

During those dark days, I never once considered divorce. In fact, I don't remember anybody even using the "D" word at our house. For one thing, there was no real reason for anybody to leave. But to be honest, there were also times when there wasn't much reason to stay . . . except for the fact that we took our marriage vows seriously. We'd promised our families and God himself to love and honor each other, for better or worse, in sickness and health, for richer or poorer, *until death*! It had been relatively easy to keep those promises when we had mostly experienced better, health, and richer. When our relationship became sick and poor, keeping the covenant we'd made would take an extra measure of grace and faith in the only One who can rekindle a flame that's almost out.

One day as I considered all this, I decided something pretty profound, if I do say so myself. A thought came to my mind as clearly as if spoken out loud by my heavenly Father: "Sick" people sometimes need a doctor.

Joe agreed to go with me for a series of counseling appointments. After meeting several times with a Christian therapist, who encouraged us to talk about our feelings, we were able to reconnect. Then we got our whole family together for a roundtable discussion. We each shared what we appreciated about each other and then how we had hurt each other. Admitting our mistakes and sins opened the door to forgiveness and growth. Little by little, one day at a time, the smoldering ashes of two cold hearts began to warm, then glow, and then burst into dancing flames, bringing warmth to everybody in the family.

Several years passed before we faced another empty nest syndrome. When we packed up Jason's things and dropped him off at college, the realization that our nest was really empty hit home with full force. As we drove away, Joe and I talked about how different our lives would be. I couldn't hold back a few tears. But that evening we settled on our sofa, put on some '50s music, and started a fire—and I don't mean in the fireplace. Whoo ha! There's life after kids.

Through all the inevitable transitions, healthy relationships are not easy for a family to maintain. Like a fire in the fireplace, they take almost constant tending. And for us, the work needed to include our children. One of the benefits of family counseling is that there's no need for anybody to keep secrets. It's been good for our kids to know that a big backlog called commitment is what keeps the fire burning through the night. They also know how important it is

WHAT A WOMAN WANTS
IN A MAN—OVER TIME

ORIGINAL LIST AT AGE 22

1. Handsome
2. Charming
3. Financially successful
4. A caring listener
5. Witty
6. In good shape
7. Dresses with style
8. Appreciates the finer things
9. Full of thoughtful surprises
10. An imaginative, romantic lover

REVISED LIST AT MIDLIFE

1. Not too ugly—bald head OK
2. Doesn't drive off until I'm in the car
3. Works steadily
4. Occasionally splurges on dinner at McDonald's
5. Nods head at appropriate times when I'm talking
6. Usually remembers the punch lines of jokes
7. Is in good enough shape to rearrange the furniture
8. Usually wears shirt that covers stomach
9. Remembers to put the toilet seat down
10. Shaves on most weekends

REVISED LIST AT RETIREMENT

1. Doesn't scare small children
2. Remembers where the bathroom is
3. Doesn't require much money for upkeep
4. Snores lightly when awake
5. Doesn't forget why he's laughing
6. Is in good enough shape to stand up by himself
7. Usually wears some clothes
8. Likes soft foods
9. Remembers where he left his teeth
10. Remembers when . . .

FINAL REVISED LIST

1. Breathing[1]

to be honest, to extend forgiveness, and to appreciate the grace of God. Just knowing that marriage takes real work has helped our adult children work through some of their own cooling-off periods. Now we all help each other keep the home fires burning.

Being so involved in each other's struggles may seem impossible to some of you—there's just no spark between you and your kids. Others of you may need to mend a broken relationship with your children before you can even think about discussing their marriages. To others, being involved in each other's personal issues may be a burden too big to bear. But with every burden comes a huge blessing and some things that are downright fun.

Which reminds me of one particular time when our warm-hearted son Matt went the extra mile, or extra miles as it turned out, to help his not-very-romantic dad do something that really lit my fire.

We had volunteered to babysit our six grandchildren while he and our daughter-in-law attended a charity ball in Dallas—an occasion benefiting the Troy Aikman Foundation for children. (As a Texan and fan of the Dallas Cowboys, it would be totally inappropriate and disloyal not to mention the recipient of my kids' generosity.) Knowing their parents would be hobnobbing with Troy seemed to heighten the excitement building around Matt's house as everybody was getting ready for the evening. While Matt and Rachel donned their tuxedo and evening gown, the girls were playing dress-up. By the time we arrived, our granddaughters were decked out in sparkly dresses, feather boas, and high heel shoes several sizes too big. Matt looked handsome in his tux, and Rachel fairly glowed in her sequined dress and the fur coat she'd borrowed from me.

After a few minutes, the limousine arrived. What a car! Sleek, black Lincoln with white running lights framing the outside windows. All six kids poured out the front door and ran toward the limo. The chauffeur bowed graciously and opened the door, allowing the children to pile in and examine the car's elegant interior. I felt like a kid myself when I climbed in after them. It's not that I'd never seen a stretch limousine; it's just that, well . . . I'd never been inside one. We sank into its cushy leather seats and checked out the two ice coolers and classy stemmed glassware. A fiber-optic light show danced around the interior and mellow music floated through the fragrant air of the cabin. Wow!

Before long, Matt and Rachel emerged from the house, and we all stood in the front yard, waving good-bye. Then

Joe and I ushered the kids back inside and spent the rest of the evening taking care of their needs. By the time our son and daughter-in-law came home around midnight, we were totally exhausted, slumped on the sofa and watching TV.

We gathered our belongings and followed Matt outside. To my surprise, the limousine was still parked out front, its tall, dignified chauffeur standing at attention by the passenger door. I noticed Matt slip something into his hand and overheard him say, "Don't take them home until they've seen the stars."

For the next half hour or so, we were escorted through the city while we sipped Diet Coke from some of the prettiest glasses I'd ever seen. Eventually the driver turned down a crooked lane that led to a bluff overlooking Grapevine Lake. Pulling close to the water, he parked and pushed a button that slowly opened the moon roof. "If you stand, you can look out," he explained. "The stars are beautiful tonight."

I grinned from ear to ear, slipped the mink coat that Rachel had left in the backseat around my shoulders, and stood. Poking my head through the open roof, I noticed two barges and several cabin cruisers gliding across the placid waters. A couple of them blew their foghorns. Apparently the limo was making quite a splash with the boaters nearby. I waved—not the silly, girlfriend hand flap that I usually offer, but a slow, arm-twisting wave, like that of the pageant winners I'd seen in the Rose Bowl Parade. A flurry of applause erupted from the yacht near the shore. I'm pretty sure they thought I was Julia Roberts. But, of course, I don't know that for certain.

After Joe and I located the Big Dipper and the North Star, we were ready to go home. We'd had as much fun as two old folks can handle in one night. But as I nestled my graying head on my pillow and pulled the comforter up to my chin, I found myself back in that limo with stars twinkling overhead and the moon casting its silvery light across my husband's face.

I turned toward him for a goodnight kiss and heard his deep, measured breathing followed by little puffs of air as he exhaled. Though I was too pooped to toss even a tiny bit of kindling his way, the embers of well-seasoned love glowed warmly in my heart.

PART 5

The Grandparent Groove

15

Finding the Get Up and Go

ACCEPTING THE CHALLENGES HANDS-ON

To keep the heart unwrinkled, to be hopeful, kindly, cheerful, reverent—that is to triumph over old age.

Thomas Bailey Aldrich

I remember when my children were preschoolers how much I needed a vacation—and I don't mean a trip to Disneyland. I needed an adult time-out with people who could wipe their own noses, cut up their own food, and speak in full sentences. My friend Judy and I had a long talk about such matters one day as we walked in the woods near her house. Seems neither of us had parents who could (or would) take on the job of watching our kids, even for a weekend. So Judy and I made a resolution then and there: When our children have kids and need a break, we will be there for them. We will not become wimps!

One day, decades later, our son Matt phoned home. "Mom, we need to get away," he said. "We've planned a trip to Bar Harbor, Maine, and, well, I'm wondering if you could keep our kids for a few days?"

Now I ask you, how could I, gracious grandmother that I am, say no?

Their brood consisted of three little chicks: Luke, six; Connor, four; and Mary Catherine, fifteen months. As their appointed time of departure neared, I thought about the cute antics of my grandsons and the charming smile of our toddler, and I could hardly wait to get those kids on my lap. I envisioned sunny days filled with warm hugs and sticky kisses and evenings of storytelling with squeaky-clean, pajama-clad kids sitting in rapt attention.

This would be like a vacation for me too, I thought. Five days away from my usual routine, just playing with the grandkids. But when I arrived at their house, it didn't take five minutes for me to realize this trip would be no vacation! On the other hand, neither would I be bored. I definitely would not be bored.

After I deposited my luggage in the guest room, I looked over the kids' schedules—complicated plans printed on an official-looking calendar with maps and a time chart attached. Their activities included three carpools, two soccer practices, and two soccer games. For the first time since I'd signed up for this tour of duty, I felt a bit apprehensive. Later, as I watched those precious children scuffling on the living room floor, I felt weak in the knees and wondered, can I really do all this?

Early the next morning their parents flew the coop, the chicks hopped out of their nest, and the funny farm began.

During the following days, I, of necessity, mastered some coping skills, which I now offer to fellow grandparents with my blessing.

My first suggestion is, well, *Just say yes!* It's a grandparent's right! There are many times that we grown-ups must say no. After all, when we've been left in charge, we don't want our children coming home to a sick or bandaged baby. But there are other times that we almost automatically say no when yes would work equally well. For example, one sugar-loaded jolt of caffeine will not do permanent damage to a kid, especially if he or she is getting ready to play in a large open field. On Tuesday evening, I had my first opportunity to just say yes.

Luke had soccer practice at 5:30. We scarfed down TV dinners, gathered Luke's gear—shorts, shirt, shoes, socks, shin guards, and ball—and were heading for the door when suddenly he bellowed, "Wait, I need to take some water!"

No problem! I knew exactly where to find his water bottle. Mary Catherine had removed it from the cabinet near the sink, and I'd put it back at least a dozen times throughout the day. I fumbled through the shelves, but the water bottle was not there.

"Where's Luke's water bottle?" I yelled. Luke and Connor shrugged their shoulders and helplessly turned their palms up. Mary Catherine grinned. Then Luke seized the opportunity to get something he really wanted.

With a voice as smooth as chocolate milk, he asked, "Grandma Gracie, since grandmothers are supposed to spoil their grandchildren, may I take a Coke?"

I stood speechless for a moment or two, thinking this kid was really slick! Then I answered, "Sure, grab one for everybody!" Three happy kids and one gullible grandma flew out the door and arrived at soccer practice just in time.

My second suggestion is *Take vitamins*. When a fifty-something woman has sole responsibility for a gaggle of grandkids, physical challenges are inevitable. Hence, a handful of mega-vitamins taken at the beginning of each day is strongly advised. I found my physical elasticity stretched to the limit on Wednesday evening when our son phoned home with what sounded like a simple request: "Mom, I need my identification badge. Would you send it by overnight mail?"

"Sure," I said, "no problem!"

The next morning after Luke left for school, I found Matt's badge, put it in an envelope, helped Connor buckle up in the backseat of the car, buckled Mary Catherine in her car seat, loaded the stroller in the trunk, and backed out of the driveway, wondering which direction to go.

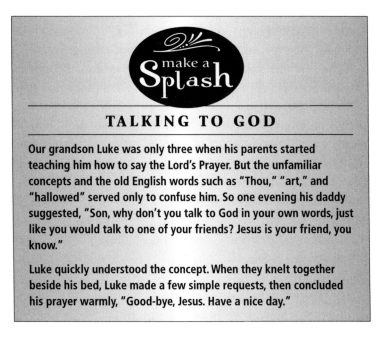

make a Splash

TALKING TO GOD

Our grandson Luke was only three when his parents started teaching him how to say the Lord's Prayer. But the unfamiliar concepts and the old English words such as "Thou," "art," and "hallowed" served only to confuse him. So one evening his daddy suggested, "Son, why don't you talk to God in your own words, just like you would talk to one of your friends? Jesus is your friend, you know."

Luke quickly understood the concept. When they knelt together beside his bed, Luke made a few simple requests, then concluded his prayer warmly, "Good-bye, Jesus. Have a nice day."

After twenty minutes, I located the post office, parked the car, and started unloading. Connor helped me get the stroller and unfolded it while I unbuckled Mary Catherine from her car seat. I secured her in the stroller, took Connor's hand, and managed to get them lined up inside. After ten minutes of waiting, I learned that Bar Harbor is "off the U.S. Post Office's beaten path," so their "overnight" mail would not, technically speaking, be delivered overnight. I shoved the envelope back in my purse and headed for the door.

Back outside, I undid everything I had previously done: unstrapped the baby, lifted her out of the stroller, buckled her snugly in the car seat, helped Connor buckle up, folded the stroller, loaded it back in the car, and decided to drive to Federal Express, where overnight means overnight. Surely things would move quickly in a place with "Express" on the door.

Once there, I decided to forgo the stroller. Hoisting Mary Catherine onto my hip, I grabbed Connor's hand and trudged inside. I plopped Mary Catherine on the counter and began filling out the required forms. She grabbed my pencil. When I moved her little dimpled hand, she crumpled the papers. Clearly this situation called for a change in strategy. So I put Mary Catherine on the floor next to Connor and pinned her to the counter with my spraddled legs.

"What's your return address?" the clerk asked. For the life of me, I couldn't remember my son's address. "How 'bout the phone number?" Noticing my blank look, she shuffled through a drawer and handed me the telephone directory. Before I could find the right page, the clerk shook her head and announced, "Lady, your baby's walking out the door!"

I whirled and ran. As soon as Mary Catherine stepped through the open door and onto the sidewalk, I swooped her into my arms like a hawk snatching a runaway chick. Mary Catherine grinned. Obviously, I would need that stroller after all.

With Connor in tow, I went back to the car, unfolded the stroller, secured the baby on board, marched back into the office, and finished the paperwork. Then I loaded the kids, drove home, put my feet up, and downed another handful of vitamins, along with two Extra Strength Migraine Excedrin.

In addition to the physical challenges we grandparents face when we tangle with our progeny, there are mental and emotional frustrations as well. Hence my third suggestion, which, alas, I learned the hard way: *Never argue with a six-year-old!* It takes a determined decision on our part, since we older folk have so much wisdom and practical information to dispense. But we must remember the value of allowing those precious little ones to fail. Besides that, it feels so good to have them eventually admit that you were right after all.

It was Saturday morning when I made the mistake of trying to match wits with Luke, a kid who had just started first grade. How naive of me! His soccer game was scheduled on field no. 6. I knew this for sure because his mother had carefully pointed out that the kids would not be playing on their usual field. If only she'd explained this to Luke.

In the parking lot, before I could even begin the interminable unfolding of the stroller, Luke surveyed the various playing fields and loudly pronounced, "Grandma Gracie, this is the wrong field."

"The schedule listed field no. 6," I said confidently as I fastened the stroller's safety belt securely around Mary Catherine's tummy and grabbed Connor's hand.

"But we always play on that field!" he said, pointing toward one on the other side of the road.

"Well, today it's no. 6." Then, just to silence all arguments, I added, "Your mother said so."

But Luke would not give up easily. He countered, "My coach said field no. 5."

My feathers bristled. "Luke, you're wrong. Now let's get to field no. 6!"

As we trudged across the parking lot, I overheard him grumble, "Well, I believe my coach!"

I'm ashamed to admit this, but I couldn't stifle a very childish comeback. "Well, I believe *your mother*!" I took a deep breath and pushed the heavily loaded stroller up-hill toward my choice of playing field. Luke tagged along behind.

When we rounded the corner, Luke spotted his teammates on field no. 6—just as I had said. Before he darted onto the field, I got down on his level, and I don't mean just physically. We faced off nose to nose like two preschoolers tugging on one lollipop. I was right, dad-gum it, and I wanted him to admit it! After a few moments of awkward silence, I draped my arm around his shoulders, looked directly into his eyes, and asked, "Luke, were you wrong?"

He shifted uncomfortably, kicked the dirt, and answered, "I think my coach was wrong."

With that, I was ready to concede defeat. But I'd no sooner turned around than I felt a tug on my sleeve. As I turned back, I looked into Luke's doe-brown eyes pooling with tears and heard his sweet voice saying, "I'm sorry, Grandma Gracie."

Looking into his face, all my frustration vanished. We grinned at each other, and I patted him on the back. Then I watched him take his place on the field, his cleats kicking up little clouds of dust as he ran. *This kid's more than smooth, I thought; he's absolutely charming and totally irresistible.*

Even though we grandparents adore our little ones and think their antics are precious, we must admit we need divine help to deal with them. Which brings me to my fourth, and most important, grandparenting tip: *Realize you can't do it alone.*

Each evening I bathed the kids and dressed them in soft, footed pajamas. Then we huddled on the bottom bunk in their bedroom for stories, hugs, and prayers.

Before lights out on our last night together, Luke quoted the verses I'd been helping him memorize from the Lord's Prayer. He folded his hands under his chin and began in a reverent tone, "Our Father, which art in heaven, hallowed be Thy name. . . ." As he spoke the familiar words, it seemed to me that our heavenly Father was listening nearby.

I whispered, "Lord, you are my daily source of strength and wisdom. Thank you for being faithful." Just as I prayed for his guidance as a mother, I sought it even more as a grandmother.

When Luke finished his prayer, Mary Catherine jabbered hers, and Connor added, "God bless Grandma Gracie." I belted out a loud and heartfelt "Amen!" Tucking the covers under their chins, I kissed my grandchildren goodnight and cherished the priceless moments together.

The next morning, when our son and daughter-in-law returned home, I welcomed them enthusiastically with a renewed sense of appreciation. (And, I might add, a new understanding of my parents' decision not to keep grandchildren overnight!) "Thanks for all you do for these wonderful grandkids!" I said sincerely.

WISH FOR BETTER

Radio personality Paul Harvey once mused on how we try so hard to make things better for our kids that we make them worse. "For my grandchildren, I'd like better," he concluded. "I'd really like for them to know about hand-me-down clothes and homemade ice cream and leftover meat loaf sandwiches. I really would." Here are some of his other wishes that you can make yours . . . for good and for better:

- Hope to learn humility by being humiliated, and learn honesty by being cheated. Hope to learn to make one's own bed, mow the lawn, and wash the car.
- Wish, if at least one time, to see puppies born and the dog put to sleep.
- Hope to get a black eye fighting for something you believe in.
- Hope to have to walk uphill to school with friends, and that you live in a town where you can do it safely.
- Hope, if you want a slingshot, that your dad teaches you how to make one instead of buying one. Hope to dig in the dirt and read books, and even when you learn to use computers, that you also learn to add and subtract in your head.
- Hope to get teased by your friends when you have your first crush on a girl, and when you talk back to your mother, that you learn what Ivory soap tastes like.
- Hope to skin a knee climbing a mountain, burn a hand on the stove, and stick one's tongue on a frozen flagpole.
- Make time to sit on a porch with a grandpa and go fishing with an uncle.
- Feel sorrow at a funeral and joy during the holidays.
- Hope your mother punishes you when you throw a baseball through your neighbor's window and that she hugs you and kisses you at Christmastime when you give her a plaster mold of your hand.
- Wish for tough times and hard work, disappointment and happiness—and in all, to find the way to appreciate life.[1]

193

Then, in what may have been a moment of temporary insanity, I recalled my vow of yesteryear and added cheerfully, "Hey, next time you need help, just call Grandma!" With that, I packed up my vitamins, BENGAY ointment, and heating pad, then kissed my grandkids, waved good-bye, winced, and wobbled my way out the door.

16

Got Game?

❧

DISCOVERING THE VALUE OF PLAYFULNESS

You don't stop playing because you grow old,
you grow old because you stop playing.

Anonymous

When our son Mike was in second grade, he wrote a story called "The Rainy Day." I still have his original work preserved in a special keepsake box in my study. The story is important to me not only for its creativity but because it memorializes something special about our family and the bond we have with each other—a bond that was created, at least in part, by the games we played when our kids were growing up. Mike's story, replete with questionable grammar and misspelled words, follows:

The Rainy Day

The rain was poaring and the boy and girl were running as fast as they could run. When they got to the house they put on dry shooes. Then they said, Lets stay in. So they got out a game. The name of the game was Up the Tree and the ages was 7 to 11.

Then it stopped raining and they went out to play. The boy climbed a tree. And the girl played in the playhouse. The dog was a sleep. The mother was baking cookies. And, the name of the cookies was chocolate-chip. And at that time it started to rain. And they went home again.

The End

As I read Mike's story today, more than two decades since it was written, it reminds me once again of the warmth that filled our home (most of the time), not only on rainy days, but on sweltering summer days and cold, dreary winter days. I can still smell the chocolate chip cookies baking in the oven and feel the excitement of our little boys as they opened up their favorite board game and distributed the pieces around the table. Our sons loved to play with each other, but the games became even more fun (and, I might add, a lot less competitive) when the whole family got involved.

The game-playing tradition that began when our babies were barely old enough to play patty-cake continued even during our boys' teen years and is still going on now that we have grandchildren. For us, playing games has been therapy, comfort, and just plain fun. But more importantly, playing together has strengthened our family ties, creating memories that will last a lifetime. To this day, Mike still likes rainy days at home, board games, and chocolate chip cookies.

When he comes home for a visit, bringing two little boys of his own, they all head for the kitchen to see if anything is baking. Then the kids run to the toy box to pick out their favorite game. These days the name of the cookies might be Pillsbury Ready To Bake, and there are some newfangled additions to our game chest I don't totally get. But the passion for play hasn't changed that much. First thing I know, one of the kids is tugging on my sleeve, begging, "Play with me, Grandma Gracie. Will you please?"

Now I have to admit a kid's timing is almost always somewhat off. It never fails—as soon as I pull out all my ingredients to bake a cake or sit down with a cup of coffee for some adult conversation, Montana shows up looking for a buddy to play with. But if we grown-ups are not careful, we'll let our busy schedules rob us of some of life's most precious moments. So I usually respond with Scarlett-O'Hara-like reasoning, "Let's play! I'll think about cooking and cleaning tomorrow."

For most of us grandmas, there's nothing more enjoyable than playing with our grandchildren, especially when we realize we're helping them grow socially and develop important abilities. Playing games helps our little ones acquire skills in listening and observation as well as the capacity to follow directions and solve problems. Games also teach significant concepts and provide valuable information.

Montana, Mike's five-year-old, loves to play Sorry. There are times when I've thought the game a bit too competitive, and at other times a bit too, well . . . heartless. I just hate to land on a square that Montana's game piece occupies. When I do, it sends the little guy back "home," and he has to start all over again.

There are occasions when Montana seems to regret landing on my square as well, but usually he has no qualms about sending me back home. He giggles, stomps his feet, and claps as if he really loves to get the best of his grandma. (See what I mean about being too competitive?) I remember one occasion when I seriously doubted the validity of playing such an out-to-get-you game when Montana learned a valuable lesson.

I counted out eleven places on the game board and realized I would land on a square occupied by my precious grandson who'd already tripped back home several times during our game-playing marathon. So I decided to fudge a bit. "Oops," I blurted, "I miscounted. Let me do that again." I moved my piece backward to a spot I knew was more than eleven places behind Montana's piece and then recounted. I had just done the compassionate thing, sparing him the agony of loss.

At least that's what I thought. But when we concluded the game and were putting the pieces away, Montana said, "Well, I was the winner today. I won all three games." He paused, looked through me with his big, brown eyes, and added, "But I really only won two."

My heart beat fast, like it used to do when I was a kid and my mother had just caught me fabricating a story. I didn't know whether to fess up or feign innocence when he cleared his throat and said, "Grandma Gracie, I know you cheated!"

Well, that did it! What could I do but apologize? "I'm sorry, Montana," I said. "I just felt sorry for you." Then I grinned and said, "Maybe that's why the game is called Sorry, huh? I won't let you win again." And to this day, I've not gone easy on that kid! His Sorry skills have improved so much, there are times I wish he'd miscount a few squares in my favor.

MAKE THE MOST WITH GRANDKIDS

You'll discover how to enjoy your grandkids more as they learn important concepts and skills with a few games. Try these:

FOR PRESCHOOLERS

- **Old Maid** (and other card games)—Matching, counting, skill in handling small objects
- **Chutes and Ladders**—Rewards and consequences
- **Hi Ho Cherry O**—Simple counting, number recognition, social skills
- **Bob the Builder**—Value of teamwork, strong friendships, diligence, self-esteem, enjoying your work
- **Operation**—Hand-eye coordination, identification of parts of the anatomy

FOR ELEMENTARY SCHOOLERS

- **Lincoln Logs**—Manual skills, creativity, handling small objects
- **Lite Bright**—Color, creativity in design, artistic expression
- **Sorry**—Sportsmanship, following directions, fairness
- **Battleship**—Developing memory and the ability to follow directions
- **Pick Up Sticks**—Helps with concentration and coordination

FOR TWEENS & TEENS

- **Monopoly**—Handling money, buying and selling, decision making skills
- **Scrabble**—Love for words, strategic thinking skills, uses numbers and mathematics
- **Checkers or Chess**—concentration, focus, memory, patience
- **Scattergories**—Sounds of alphabet and word skills
- **Balderdash**—Word skills, definition, vocabulary, meaning of words

Not all the games we play provide such character-building experiences—some are just-for-fun games that actually have very little redeeming value; others border on the ridiculous. Such is another of Montana's favorites—a classic card game called Old Maid. It's a simple game that often leaves me holding the dreaded card, while Montana hoots and hollers as he dubs me the Old Maid.

Of course, I don't hesitate offering a snappy comeback: "That woman is definitely not me!" Montana knows full well I'm not the rocking chair type. In fact, I take great pride in being "off my rocker" and into mischief and fun! Nevertheless, a verbal tug-of-war ensues between Montana and me until one of us gives up and deals the cards again.

It's never too soon to engage your grandchildren in games. Even babies benefit from play. They relax when they hear your playful tone of voice and feel your arms around them. When they become toddlers, game playing teaches them motor skills as well as how to express themselves and how to handle their emotions.

Myles, Montana's three-year-old brother, has a more contemplative personality. He likes working puzzles, stacking blocks, and making houses from Lincoln Logs. Even though Myles's game of choice always includes lots of pieces (which we eventually have to pick up, sort, and put away), I see the benefit of playing games like these. The tiny pieces keep his hands busy so we can talk. It's during our talks that I really learn what's going on in his quickly developing mind.

One day, just after he checked on the cookies browning nicely in the oven, he climbed into a chair and then up on top of our game table. He plopped down next to the pieces of a new puzzle, which I'd spread and organized according to color.

"Want to help me put this together?" I asked.

"Sure," little Myles said as he fingered the odd-shaped pieces. He selected one with bright blue edges. While he pushed the piece in place at the top of the picture and put other pieces into the proper spaces, he jabbered continually. Eventually the puzzle was almost finished. There was one last piece on the table, one final space to be filled.

Myles snatched the piece off the table and started to put it in the remaining hole, grinning impishly as he gloried in the triumph of placing the last piece. But fitting the odd-shaped piece in place proved too complicated a task for his chubby little hands to handle. No matter which way he turned the piece or how hard he pushed, it simply would not slide into place. As I watched quietly, his internal engines were building up enough steam to power a small locomotive. He turned red in the face and started shoving and pounding on the piece—all the while muttering indistinguishable words under his breath.

Finally one word took shape and came out loud and clear: "Oh, Gaahhhhddd!" For some reason, hearing my sweet toddler take the Lord's name in vain struck me funny. Of course, I didn't let him know it. I slapped my hand over my mouth and ran into the other room. After a few moments, I regained my composure, returned, and put my arms around his tiny shoulders. Taking his hand in mine, I helped him fit the odd-shaped piece into the empty space. Sensing a teachable moment, I zinged in the moral lesson for the day by saying, "Myles, it's not right to say God's name when you're angry."

"I'm sawy, Gamma Gacie," he muttered. Then he grinned shyly and slipped his arms around my neck. As I held him close, my heart filled with joy, for I realized this precious

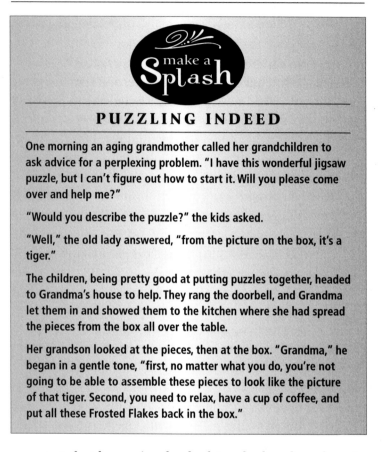

make a Splash

PUZZLING INDEED

One morning an aging grandmother called her grandchildren to ask advice for a perplexing problem. "I have this wonderful jigsaw puzzle, but I can't figure out how to start it. Will you please come over and help me?"

"Would you describe the puzzle?" the kids asked.

"Well," the old lady answered, "from the picture on the box, it's a tiger."

The children, being pretty good at putting puzzles together, headed to Grandma's house to help. They rang the doorbell, and Grandma let them in and showed them to the kitchen where she had spread the pieces from the box all over the table.

Her grandson looked at the pieces, then at the box. "Grandma," he began in a gentle tone, "first, no matter what you do, you're not going to be able to assemble these pieces to look like the picture of that tiger. Second, you need to relax, have a cup of coffee, and put all these Frosted Flakes back in the box."

moment that began in play had touched a place deep in my toddler's soul.

Games not only open doors of communication between grandmas and their toddlers, but they help us communicate with teenagers as well. In our high-tech society, it's hard to imagine teenagers playing board games. But if the circumstances are right and there's no fast-moving entertainment available, sometimes a simple game will do.

I remember one weekend in particular when Joe and I and our two teenage sons, Matt and Mike, were vacationing in our cabin on the lake. While a storm raged outside, we huddled around our old Dearborn heater and started a game of Monopoly. We'd no sooner distributed the money and game pieces than lightning flashed and the lights blinked, then went off. Apparently a power failure had occurred, leaving us sitting around the table in total darkness.

Since power outages happened fairly frequently in this rural area, I knew exactly where to find a flashlight, a few candles, and some matches. Once a tiny flame started to glow, I took an antique lamp down from its decorative stand trimmed and lit the wick. With its clear glass globe in place, the lamp cast a warm glow throughout the room. Then we played until time for bed. Matt and Mike still talk about that evening. Nobody remembers who won or lost or if we even finished the game, but none of us will forget the experience of playing Monopoly by the light of that old lantern.

When recalling moments like these, most grandmothers would like to take our grandkids by the hand and step back in time to simpler, quieter days. But the reality is our offspring are growing up in the new millennium, facing difficult days made even more complicated by cell phones, beepers, headphones, computers, and video games. Since we can't retreat to days gone by, we must make the most of the moments we do have right here, right now. For some of us, that means expanding our horizons to include some high-tech toys, computer software, and video games.

Now that our oldest grandchild, Luke, is a teen, it takes more creativity on my part to stay connected to him. I watch while he puts together a model or paints action figures. At other times I pull up a chair and look over his shoulder while he plays on the computer. While it may take extra effort to spend time with my older grandchildren, the payoff is worth it. Why, just the other day Luke gave me a big hug and said I was "one rad grandma" (I think that means radical, which is a compliment!).

Recently Mike, Jeanna, Montana, and Myles arrived for an overnight visit. I heard the back door open and glanced up as Montana rounded the corner into the living room, where I was sitting on the sofa. When he realized I was talking on the phone, he stopped dead in his tracks and waited for me to push the Off button. The big grin on his face spoke volumes to me—I'm here, Grandma! I love you, Grandma! (I can read anything I want into my nonverbal messages, okay?) I couldn't wait to give my precious grandboy a big hug.

As I wrapped my arms around him, his very first words were, "What do you want to play?"

I couldn't hold back the laughter as I turned my palms up and said, "Whatever!" Then I quickly added, "You pick the game; I'll get the cookies."

17

Pushing Away from the Dock

❧

MAKING THE INEVITABLE TRANSITIONS

Maybe the way in which we travel and the attitude we have
while making our way through life is more important than
reaching our destination. Or could it be that in God's sight,
the way actually is the destination?

Corrie ten Boom

One day after school, my five-year-old grandson,
Montana, gathered a few pieces of red construction
paper, a lace paper doily, scissors, and a handful
of markers. Then he began working on what seemed to be
a rather complicated project. Seated at the kitchen table, he
cut and pasted, colored with the markers, and occasionally
wiped his forehead with the back of his hand. Obviously he

was creating a valentine. His mother—my daughter-in-law Jeanna—not wanting to spoil her child's surprise, tried to be inconspicuous as she observed.

Finally Montana completed the project, asked for an envelope, and then slipped his handmade expression of love inside. He picked up the black marker and, with a satisfied expression on his upturned face, asked, "Mom, how do you spell Mrs. Wray?"

Suddenly Jeanna understood the valentine was not for her, but for Montana's kindergarten teacher. A flush of emotion swept over her as she realized her son was growing up. The reality hit hard. Montana's world was enlarging to include other adults whom he respected—and loved.

On one hand, Jeanna was pleased about her son's social growth, especially when she thought about the child's sensitivity and thoughtfulness. But she also felt like she was losing something precious. No longer was she the exclusive source of her son's childhood training. She wondered if there would come a time when Montana would value his teacher's instruction more than his mother's. Like a video on fast forward, she imagined a scene that portrayed Montana as an independent, self-sufficient young man, and her emotions did a flip-flop. She felt deeply grateful.

Turning toward the window, she brushed away a tear. Jeanna didn't want Montana to see this display of emotion.

But Montana noticed! The lad jumped up from his place at the table. Putting his arms around his mother's waist, he hugged her tightly and said, "Mom, I love you more than anybody else in the whole world." He took a deep breath. "Mom, you have my real heart. I'm just giving Mrs. Wray a copy."

When Jeanna called to relay this story to me, I found myself swallowing hard to choke back a lump rising in my throat.

Of my six grandchildren, Montana is the most sensitive, affectionate, and kind. Almost every time we talk on the phone, he ends the conversation with a loving compliment much like the one he just gave to his mother: "You are the best grandmother in the whole world." Being the sentimental soul that I am, I can hardly keep from crying when he spouts such endearments. Hearing expressions of love coming from the mouths of our little ones is only one reason grandparenting is considered "grand."

BEWARE: GRANDMOTHER WITH PHOTOS

A fast-paced executive was hoping to get some work done on a cross-country flight. He had his laptop computer running when the lady next to him struck up a conversation. Although he had a great deal of work to attend to, he welcomed the brief interchange with this pleasant older woman. After several minutes of enjoyable conversation, the executive politely excused himself and said he must get back to his work.

The woman was apparently oblivious to the man's need to work and continued to talk. She went from one subject to the next. The businessman tried to remain polite, so he halfway listened while continuing with his work.

After nearly an hour of constant talk, the woman started digging through her purse. When she found what she was looking for, she turned to the now stressed-out executive and asked, "Did I tell you about my grandchildren?"

He quickly replied, "No, ma'am. And I really appreciate it!"

I was also fighting tears because Jeanna's feelings reminded me of some of my own mixed feelings when my little boys— including Montana's dad, Mike—were growing up. I'll never forget the first day of school the year Mike started first grade. In those days kindergarten was optional, and even though we chose to send our kids, they only attended half days at a church-sponsored program. So I just knew that first grade would be a major passage for our barely six-year-old son. As it turned out, it was more of a problem for the mother than for the child.

On that special morning, I pulled my car into a parking spot at Greenville's Bowie School and gathered my purse and keys so I could escort my children inside. But I'd no sooner opened the driver's door than I heard the back door slam and saw Mike and his older brother, Matt, making a beeline for the building. Mike looked back over his shoulder and yelled, "I know where to go, Mom. See you later." I remember wiping tears on my sleeve as I climbed back in my station wagon and drove home. The house was strangely quiet that day while I tried to adjust to being home alone. I couldn't wait until three, when I could pick up those kids and have things back to normal.

～⌒⌒

The first day of school is only the first major transition we parents face as our children grow up. We transition again when our kids reach other milestones—getting a driver's license, going on their first date, heading off to college. Some of life's transitions happen because of a parent's choice—accepting a new job, moving to a different location, or scaling down to a smaller home. Through all the changes our family has made, we've struggled, adapted, and eventually embraced the change as a new beginning with great possibilities. But

I have to admit, sometimes the struggle was long and hard while we adjusted to the various stages of life. Such struggles are the stuff of life.

"A family is a mobile—a human art form," writes Edith Schaeffer. "Within the framework of family each individual is moving, changing, growing, or declining—affecting each other intellectually, emotionally, spiritually, physically, and psychologically. The grouping of toddlers with young school-children, of ten-year-olds with teenagers, of young married couples with middle-aged couples, of grandparents with two generations coming along under them, is an amazingly real, vivid, and living mobile."[1] As the mobile of our lives moves erratically, we are not helpless victims of circumstance or products of fate. We are free to follow our hearts, make radical changes, and if need be, make a midcourse correction.

After my brother-in-law Archie had a heart attack, he and my sister Lois decided it was time to live the life they'd dreamed of. They sold their house and their business in Arlington, where they'd lived for more than twenty years, and moved to the small East Texas town of Quitman. A rambling house overlooking a placid lake in a laid-back little town seemed the perfect place to settle into a more serene lifestyle. Archie and Lois knew the move would be a major transition. Not only would they have to adjust from living in a busy metropolitan area to dwelling in suburbia, but they would be moving away from their three young adult sons, Jerry, Tommy, and Larry. Nevertheless, they were following their heart—especially Archie's! He was determined to live out his second half of life doing what he's always wanted to do: go fishing!

For the first few weeks in their new location, Archie occupied himself with making a few necessary changes, like remodeling

CONSIDER THE COSTS
OF MOTHERHOOD

The words of this anonymous mother say it well:

We are sitting at lunch one day when my daughter casually mentions that she and her husband are thinking of starting a family. "We're taking a survey," she says half-joking. "Do you think I should have a baby?"

"It will change your life," I say, carefully keeping my tone neutral.

"I know," she says. "No more sleeping in on weekends, no more spontaneous vacations . . ."

But that is not what I meant. I look at my daughter, trying to decide what to tell her. I want her to know what she will never learn in childbirth classes. I want to tell her that the physical wounds of childbearing will heal, but becoming a mother will leave her with an emotional wound so raw she will forever be vulnerable.

I consider warning her that she will never again read a newspaper without asking, "What if that had been my child?" That every plane crash and every house fire will haunt her. That when she sees pictures of starving children, she will wonder if anything could be worse than watching your child die.

I look at her carefully manicured nails and stylish suit and think that no matter how sophisticated she is, becoming a mother will reduce her to the primitive level of a bear protecting her cub. That an urgent call of "Mom!" will cause her to drop a soufflé or her best crystal without a moment's hesitation.

I feel that I should warn her that no matter how many years she has invested in her career, she will be professionally derailed by motherhood. She might arrange for child care, but one day she will

210

be going into an important business meeting and she will think of her baby's sweet smell. She will have to use every ounce of discipline to keep from running home just to make sure her baby is all right, and no matter how decisive she may be at the office, she will second-guess herself constantly as a mother.

I want to describe to my daughter the exhilaration of seeing your child learn to ride a bike. I want to capture for her the belly laugh of a baby who is touching the soft fur of a dog or cat for the first time. I want her to taste the joy that is so real it actually hurts.

My daughter's quizzical look makes me realize that tears have formed in my eyes. "You'll never regret it," I finally say. I reach across the table, squeeze my daughter's hand, and offer a silent prayer for her, and for me, and for all the mere mortal women who stumble their way into this most wonderful of callings, this blessed gift from God . . . that of being a mother.[2]

the house, reinforcing the pier, adding a boathouse, and buying a brand-new fishing boat. He couldn't have been happier.

But before long the house was finished, the boat was anchored in the new boathouse, and . . . Archie was slipping into a melancholy state. Sometimes after supper, about the time fishing should have been at its peak, Lois would find her hubby sitting on the deck, looking across the water, his eyes glazed over. One day she followed him outside and sat down. "Archie, what's bothering you?" she asked, pulling her chair close. "Why don't you ever take the boat out?"

After a long pause, he answered, "I miss the boys."

"I don't know how you could," my sister said. "At least one of them shows up here every weekend!"

But things were not the same. When they lived in Arlington, Tommy and Larry worked with Archie in their plumbing business, so they'd get together for coffee and go over work orders almost every morning. Jerry stopped by the house regularly. No wonder Archie felt lonely. Eventually living a life of leisure totally lost its appeal to this doting father. Boating and fishing were simply not much fun if he couldn't share the experience with his sons. There was nothing left to do but sell the house on the lake and go back "home."

Archie and Lois's experience helped my husband and I steady our course when we plunged into the changing tides of midlife. I knew that every phase of life has its own inherent good, its peculiar rewards. I also knew it was up to me to wade through the waves of change until my feet stood on solid ground.

One of our most difficult passages was when our boys became teens. Their new status as key-carrying, freewheeling teenagers left us feeling left out and just a tad insecure. Like releasing an arrow into the wind, we'd been forced to let go of the string we'd held on to so tightly.[3] Were our children ready to soar on their own? Would they follow the right direction and stay on target? We felt even more angst when they packed up their belongings and headed off to college.

The adjustment was especially painful when our third son, Jason, moved into a student apartment three hours away. As two aging parents and one lazy dachshund padded around on the carpeted floors of our rural home, it was entirely too quiet. We found ourselves becoming depressed and lonely. Of course, a few weeks later we discovered the myth of the empty nest. Jason showed up at our door with a huge basket of laundry, thus proving the assertion made by one of our favorite TV personalities, Bill Cosby. One day as Joe and I were watching The Cosby Show, we burst into laughter when Cosby expressed the exact sentiment: "It's not an empty nest; it's a revolving door."

For most of us, the empty nest and the revolving door syndromes occur in tandem with another of life's major passages—midlife. It's that turbulent period that some folks call "crisis time." According to one negative-thinking friend, midlife is when folks "no longer think about how long it's been since their birth, but how much time they have left to live." What a distressing way to think!

The truth is, while we may be feeling the effects of aging, most of us will have another thirty-five or forty years to keep making waves. A second adulthood. This means we have time to pick up the pieces of a career interrupted or to follow the dreams we dreamed when we were eighteen or twenty-five. Instead of having a midlife crisis, why not consider the midyears a golden opportunity? Why not, in the words of Jon Katz in his book *Running to the Mountain*, "confront change rather than react to it"?[4]

When I began wading into the midyears, I found myself a bit anxious. Okay, worried, as I wondered just what kind of tidal wave might sweep me off my feet. Then I came to a personal turning point. I simply decided not to have a crisis. Instead, I chose to pursue a dream I'd had since high school. In Act II of the drama of my life I would learn to write! For the next few months the keyboard on our home computer clicked crazily as I pecked out a story. Then I took a deep breath and mailed it to one of my favorite magazines. I wondered if just maybe they'd want to publish it. They did! Whoo ha! There is life after kids.

Mr. Katz chose to deal with midlife in another creative way. He bought a cabin atop a mountain in upstate New York, where he spent several months alone—except for his two yellow Labs—reading Thomas Merton and reflecting on his life, including his spiritual self. Katz, a journalist, author, father, and husband, had become fifty. His career in writing had "taken an uneasy turn," his wife was involved in her own career, and his daughter was leaving home for college. He wrote, "I had settled down. Any more settling and I would vanish into the mud like some fat old catfish." He simply had to get away and rethink things. During his experience on the mountain, he redefined his life, finding new meaning, becoming "a better human."

"For myself at fifty," Katz wrote, "I saw the beginning of distinct physical and emotional changes. I needed stronger prescriptions for my eyeglasses. I had plenty of energy, but for the first time, I sometimes needed to nap in the afternoon. Yet I also felt wiser, calmer, nicer. Beginning to be free of the fear and anger and disappointment that come with intense ambition, I'd started to want different things for the balance of my life."[5] He still wanted his writing to "shine" but for a different reason—for his own satisfaction rather than to impress others.

"For both Merton and me, approaching fifty was dramatic stuff," Katz writes. "The questions at stake were nothing less than how to live our remaining years, seize our remaining opportunities, chart the next set of explorations, come to some sort of reckoning with both the past and future. It also meant, for me, taking some of my last and best shots at self-discovery."[6]

As for their spiritual journeys, Katz and Merton took divergent paths. "If he needed to seek God in solitude, I needed to explore spirituality with people."[7] Jon Katz found contentment in watching his son prepare for fatherhood, in helping his daughter get ready for college, and in supporting an old friend who'd lost her partner. His midlife malaise took a radical turn as he faced the future with confidence. "The remainder of my days didn't have to constitute an inexorable rush toward aches, pensions, and retirement. How to spend them was my choice, and only mine. Shame on me if I didn't make the most of them."[8]

And shame on all of us if we get caught up in an undertow or swept away from our moorings and out to sea. For we could spend the rest of our days drifting like so much dead wood or washed up on an all-too-familiar shore. Instead, let us continue to make waves. A good way to begin is by asking a few pertinent questions.

Are you living the life you envisioned when you were twenty-five or thirty? Did your dream get washed out to sea by the stresses of everyday life? What did you promise yourself you'd do someday? Who have you become? What's really important?

The answers to these questions suggest the changes you can choose to make.

May I suggest you follow the example of my young grandson? Gather a few pieces of paper and some colored pens. It's time for you to decide who (or what) has your real heart. Then get busy charting the course of Your Life, Part Two.

Acknowledgments

First of all, thanks to my family of origin: to my mother, for her consistent love and graciousness; and to my siblings, Lois, Martha, Charles, George, and Harold. Being number five in this list brought its own special challenges and blessings, including the chance to watch the older-than-me members of our clan making waves in their unique styles. It's been fun trying to keep up with you.

Thank you to my grandchildren, Luke, Connor, Mary, Abby, Montana, and Myles. You don't mind it now, but someday you may cringe when you read about your escapades. So thank you now and always for being such cute and fun-loving kids. (I'm a grandmother; I can brag if I want to!) I love to tell your stories—to anybody who will listen.

Kudos to my three sons, Matt, Mike, and Jason. You're such good sports, even when I record your private moments and expose your bloopers and mistakes to untold millions. Okay, to untold thousands.

A special thanks to Jeanna, my daughter-in-law, a gal who, incredible as it may seem, considers me her friend. I love you like a daughter.

To my husband, Joe, I owe a huge debt of gratitude for your support and encouragement. Thanks also for always being on call as my personal computer tech, LAN administrator, and interpreter of things technical. Besides that, I love you for being secure enough to wash clothes, go shopping for groceries, and carry my purse when I'm tired. You are dear to me.

My deep appreciation to Dr. John Morris, for helping me make sense of spiritual things way over my head, for keeping me from rewriting Scripture to suit myself. Thanks also for providing support, biblical counsel, and pastoral care to our family.

Thank you to my agent, Lee Hough, and to the team at Alive Communications. You have represented me well. Thank you, Lee, for being a supportive friend and confidant as well.

A special thank you to Jeanette Thomason and the Revell team at Baker Publishing Group. Thanks for believing in me and helping me reach my goal. *Still Making Waves* is a better product than I ever dreamed possible. You are wonderful to work with.

Warm regards to Cynthia Spell-Humbert, Julie Barnhill, Ellie Kay, Brenda Waggoner, and Carol Kent. Your friendship and words of encouragement kept me sane as I waded into rather deep waters this year. Also, a special thanks to several girlfriends who have been "making waves" with me for more than two decades: Carolyn Johnson, Carol Lawson, Fran Sandin, Vern Warden, and Judy Shaver. May we keep swimming upstream together for another decade or two.

Lastly, thank you to Rachel St. John Gilbert for last-minute editorial help. You are much appreciated.

Notes

Chapter 1 Launching into New Depths

1. "What is Love," Broadband Reports, www.broadbandreports.com/forum/remark,9516774~mode=flat?hilite=.

Chapter 2 Where Have All the Grown-Ups Gone?

1. Erma Bombeck, *Forever, Erma* (Kansas City, MO: Andrews McKeel, 1996), 73.

2. Becky Freeman, *Peanut Butter Kisses and Mud Pie Hugs* (Eugene, OR: Harvest House, 2003), 91–93.

Chapter 3 All I Really Need to Know I Learned from Girlfriends

1. "All I Ever Needed to Know I Learned from My Girlfriends," Simply Family, www.simplyfamily.com (site has been discontinued).

2. Ecclesiastes 4:9–12.

Chapter 4 Over the Hill and On a Roll

1. Psalm 19:1.

2. "Might as Well Dance," Jane Ellen homepage, www.janeellen.com/musings/dance.html.

Chapter 5 Archaeologists Know the Best Dirt

1. Matthew 14:27.
2. "Only in America," Dang Good Jokes, September 24, 2003, www .danggoodjokes.com/why.

Chapter 6 Well-Aged Wisdom

1. Luke 10:2.
2. Beginning of Christianity—Unbelievable Grace, homepage, www .beginning-of-Christianity.com.
3. 2 Timothy 3:16
4. Hebrews 4:12
5. John 14:6.
6. John 15:15.
7. "Aging Fast," Send 4 Fun, www.send4fun.com/pages/agingfast/ agingfast.cfm.
8. Colossians 3:16.

Chapter 7 God Is Not Finished with Me Yet!

1. Timothy Newman, "Shaking Old Habits," *Guideposts*, April 1994, 16–17.
2. Proverbs 16:9.
3. Barbara Johnson, *Leaking Laffs Between Pampers and Depends* (Nashville: Word, 2000), 158–59.
4. Psalm 139:16.

Chapter 8 Navigating Troubled Waters

1. Jane Filgo, "Twinkies, Root Beer, and God," July 12, 2000, personal email.
2. Hebrews 12:15.
3. 1 John 4:18.
4. 1 Peter 4:12–13.

Chapter 9 I'm Out of My Mind—Be Back in Five Minutes

1. Philippians 4:6–7 Phillips.

2. Adapted from Lisa Birnbach, Ann Hodgman, Patricia Marx, and David Owen, *1003 Great Things about Getting Older* (New York: MJF Books, 1997).

Chapter 10 If Only I Could Remember My Ginkgo

1. Romans 8:28.
2. "My Affliction," Wit and Wisdom, December 11, 1998, www .witandwisdom.org/archive/19981211.htm.
3. Cherie Berkley, M.S., "Is Your Memory Normal?" WebMD Feature, March 28, 2004, www.mywebmd.com/content/Article/83/97613.htm.

Chapter 11 The Bite of the Sandwich Generation

1. AARP, "Grandparenting," 2004, www.aarp.org/confacts/grand-parents/pdf/G_Census_Table_1.pdf.
2. AARP, "Life Answers: Caregiving Homepage," 2004, ww.aarp.org/ life/caregiving.
3. "Random Thoughts," Deb's Fun Pages, www.debsfunpages.com/ thoughts2.htm.

Chapter 12 Keeping Both Oars in the Water

1. George Carlin, "How to Stay Young," Arthritis Insight, November 5, 2003, www.arthritisinsight.com/fun/jokes/g.html.

Chapter 13 We're in the Same Boat

1. Romans 14:1 Message.
2. Becky Freeman, Susan Duke, Rebecca Barlow Jordan, Gracie Malone, and Fran Caffey Sandin, *Courage for the Chicken Hearted* (Tulsa, OK: Honor Books, 1999), 197.
3. 1 Corinthians 12:11 Message.
4. 1 Corinthians 12:14–18 Message.

Chapter 14 Snow on the Rooftop and Fire in the Furnace

1. "What a Woman Wants in a Man," Relationship Humor, www.the romantic.com/humor/wantinaman.htm.

Chapter 15 Finding the Get Up and Go

1. Paul Harvey, "For My Grandchildren I Want Something Better," Jan's Joyous Jungle, www.jansjoyousjungle.com/paulharvey.html.

Chapter 17 Pushing Away from the Dock

1. Edith Schaeffer, *What Is a Family?* (Old Tappan, NJ: Revell, 1975), 18.

2. "Do You Think I Should Have a Baby?" New Life Community Church, www.new-life.net/parent19.htm.

3. Psalm 127:4.

4. Jon Katz, *Running to the Mountain: A Journey of Faith and Change* (New York: Villard Books, 1999), 131.

5. Ibid., 156.

6. Ibid., 173.

7. Ibid.

8. Ibid., 174.

Gracie Malone is an author, magazine contributor, and speaker, who lives in Grapevine, Texas, with her husband, Joe. They have three children and six grandchildren.

She's the author of *Off My Rocker: Grandparenting Ain't What It Used to Be* and has contributed to several other books, including Women of Faith's *She Who Laughs, Lasts.* Her articles have appeared in *Discipleship Journal, Decision, Women Alive, Christian Parenting Today, HomeLife, Celebrate Life,* and *Moody* magazines; one feature won the Best Article Award at the 1997 Florida Christian Writer's Conference.

When not writing, Gracie is a Bible study teacher, Precept leader, and much-loved speaker for women's conferences and retreats.

Speak Up with Confidence, a speaker's bureau managed by Gene and Carol Kent, handles her speaking ministry. For booking information, go online to www.speakupinc@aol.com, or call 1-888-870-7719.

You can find Gracie online at www.graciemalone.com, by email at gracie@graciemalone.com, or by phone/fax at (817) 488-2317.